THE
EVERYTHING®
MAZES
BOOK

Lose yourself in hours of fun!

Charles Timmerman

Founder of Funster.com

Adams Media
Avon, Massachusetts

Dedicated to Tenzig who was with me
in the early years and still seems near.

Publishing Director: Gary M. Krebs
Associate Managing Editor: Laura M. Daly
Associate Copy Chief: Brett Palana-Shanahan
Associate Production Editor: Casey Ebert

Director of Manufacturing: Susan Beale
Associate Director of Production:
  Michelle Roy Kelly
Cover Design: Paul Beatrice, Matt LeBlanc,
  Erick DaCosta
Design and Layout: Heather Barrett,
Brewter Brownville, Colleen Cunningham,
Jennifer Oliveira

Published by Adams Media, an F+W Publications Company
57 Littlefield Street
Avon, MA 02322
www.adamsmedia.com

ISBN 10: 1-59337-638-3
ISBN 13: 978-1-59337-638-3
Printed in the United States of America.

J   I   H   G   F   E   D   C   B   A

This publication is designed to provide accurate and authoritative information with regard to the subject matter covered. It is sold with the understanding that the publisher is not engaged in rendering legal, accounting, or other professional advice. If legal advice or other expert assistance is required, the services of a competent professional person should be sought.

—From a *Declaration of Principles* jointly adopted by a
Committee of the American Bar Association and a Committee of Publishers and Associations

Many of the designations used by manufacturers and sellers to distinguish their product are claimed as trademarks. Where those designations appear in this book and Adams Media was aware of a trademark claim, the designations have been printed with initial capital letters.

This book is available at quantity discounts for bulk purchases.
For information, please call 1-800-289-0963.

Contents

Acknowledgments

Thanks to each of the half a million or so people who have visited my Web site, *www.funster.com*, to play word games and puzzles. You are the inspiration for this book.

Much appreciation goes to my agent Jacky Sach, whose e-mail from out of the blue started me down this amusing path of writing puzzle books.

I am truly grateful to the people at Adams Media for providing this opportunity. In particular, the mazes look even better thanks to technical help from Matt LeBlanc. It was a pleasure working with my editors Gina Chaimanis and Kate Burgo.

But most of all thanks to Suzanne and Calla, you are both a-maze-ing!

Introduction

Deep in a maze on the island of Crete lived the Minotaur: half man, half bull, and most fearsome mythical monster. Enter young Theseus, the greatest of the Greek heroes who vowed to enter the maze and slay the beast. But first he fell in love with the fair Ariadne who had brains to match Theseus' strength. She provided Theseus with a simple tool: a silk thread to unwind so that he would never be lost in the maze. The idea worked great, the Minotaur was killed, and Theseus and Ariadne lived happily ever after (well, sort of).

You might not have as much at stake in solving these mazes as Theseus, but the idea is roughly the same. And, like Theseus, you can use Ariadne's technique to keep from getting hopelessly lost in a maze. Just substitute a pencil line for the silk thread. When you come upon a dead end, retrace your way back to where you made a choice of paths and take the alternative route. When you first come to a decision point, mark it with an X to make the retracing easier. Eventually you will find your way through any of these mazes. All shapes and sizes of mazes await you here. Some of them can be solved quickly, while others will demand more concentration. So go ahead, immerse yourself and get lost in these mazes. But remember: never give up if you find yourself at a dead end or the Minotaur might get you!

Diamond 1

Solution on page 230

Diamond 2

Solution on page 230

Hourglass 1

Solution on page 230

Hourglass 2

Solution on page 230

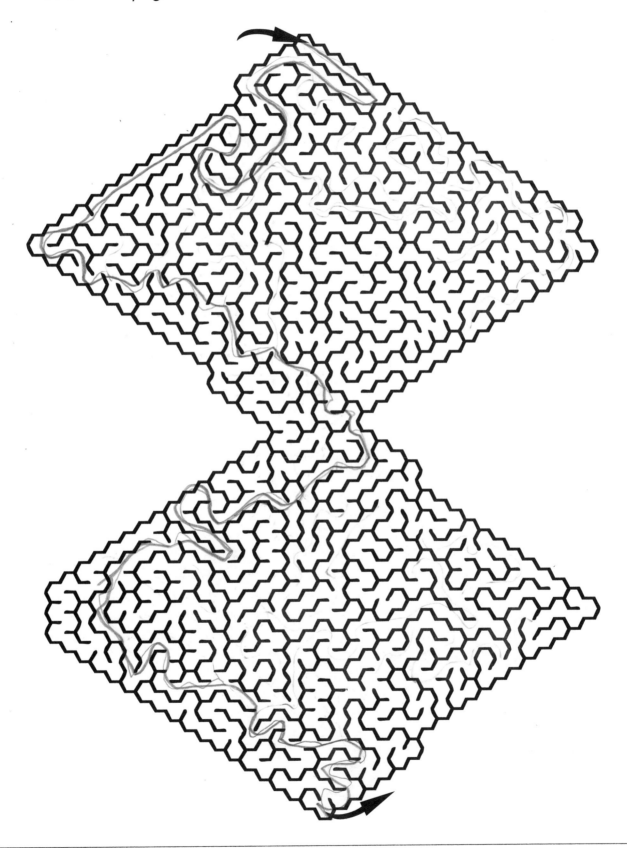

Hourglass 3

Solution on page 231

Double Diamond 1

Solution on page 231

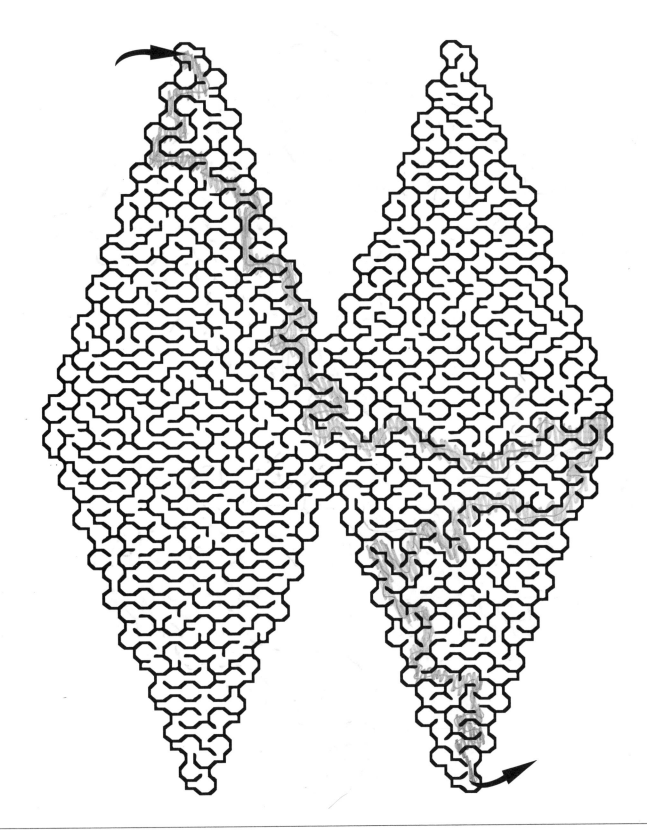

Double Diamond 2

Solution on page 231

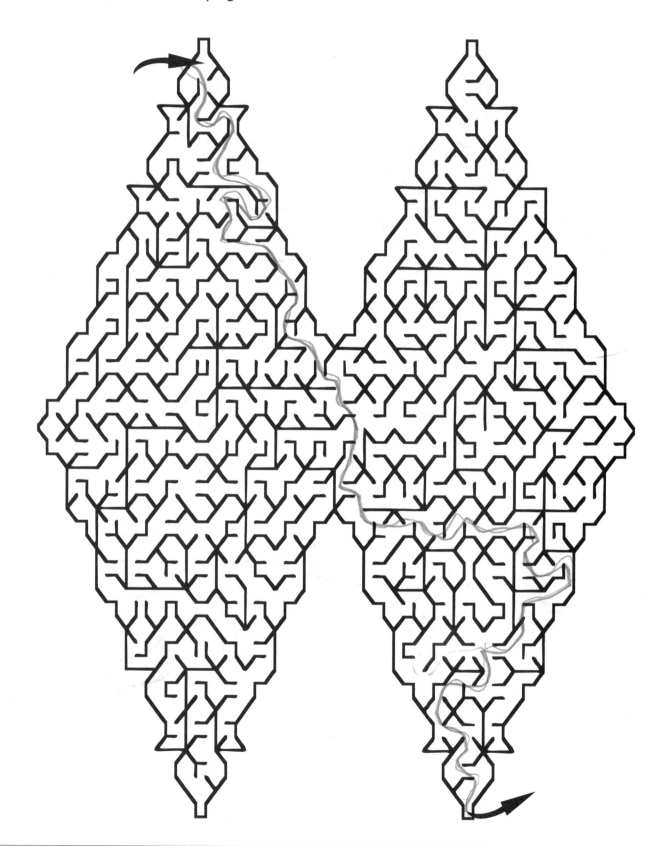

Argyle 1

Solution on page 231

Argyle 3

Solution on page 232

Doughnut 1

Solution on page 232

Doughnut 2

Solution on page 232

Circle 1

Solution on page 233

Circle 2

Solution on page 233

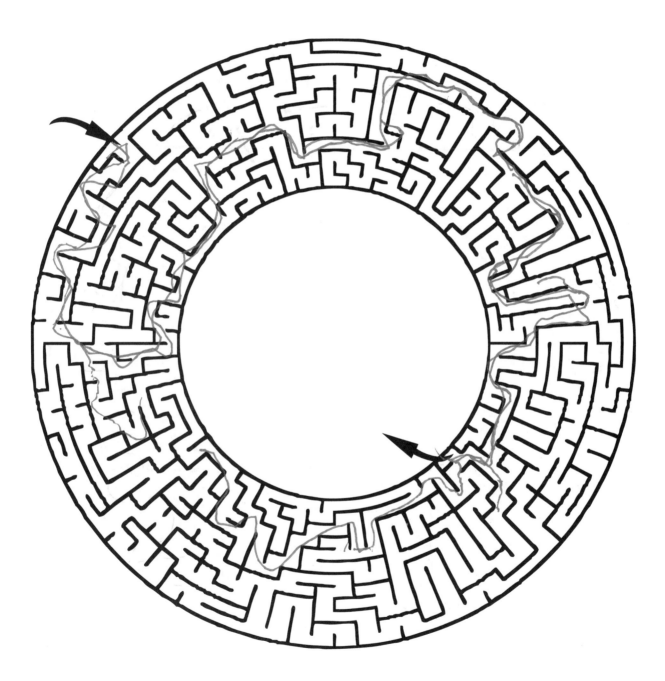

Ball 1

Solution on page 233

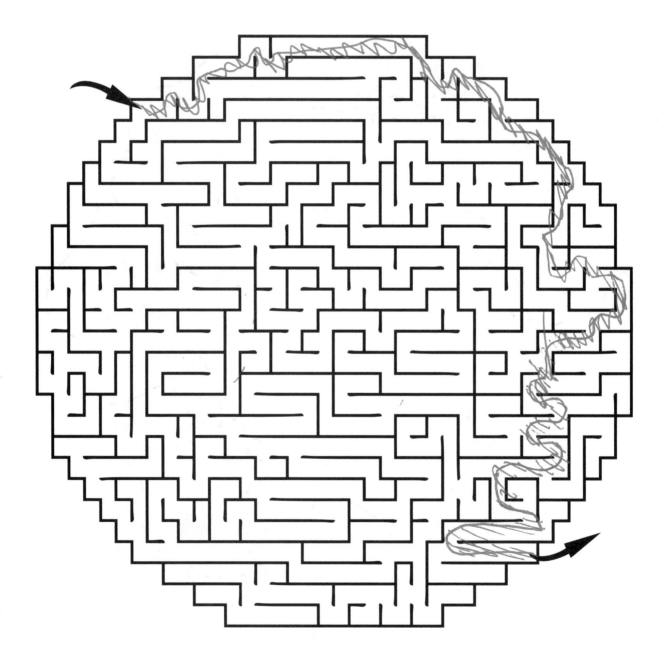

Ball 2

Solution on page 233

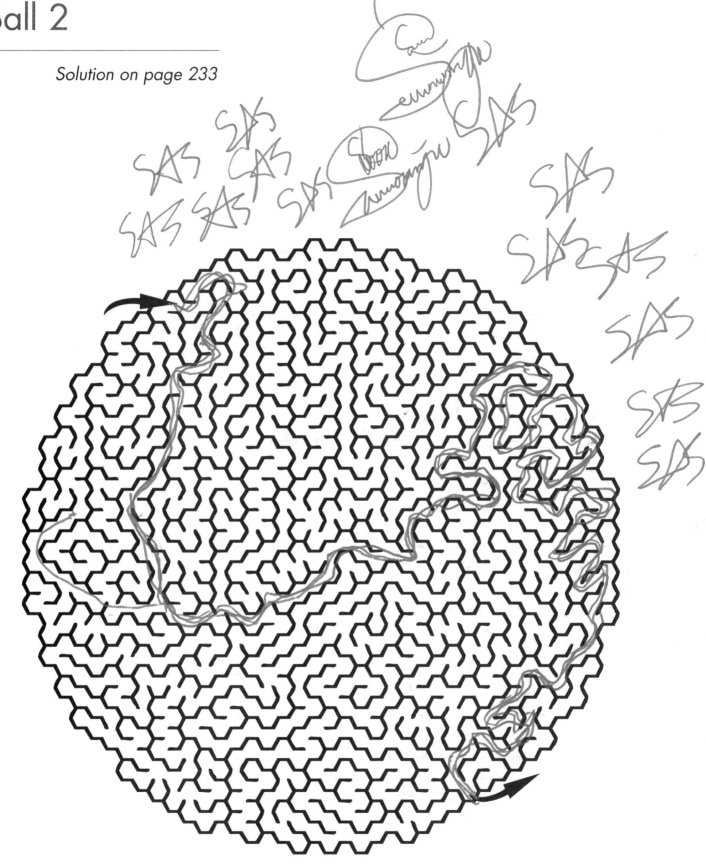

Iris 1

Solution on page 234

Iris 2

Solution on page 234

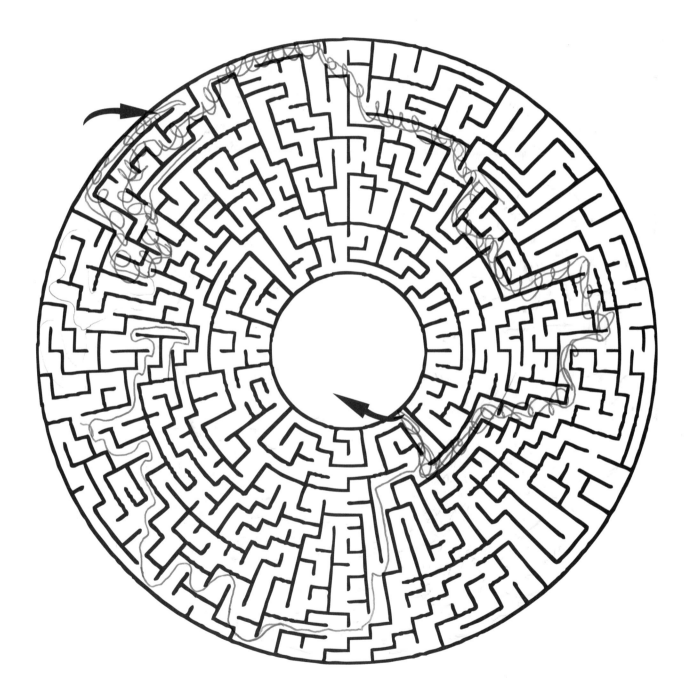

Oval 1

Solution on page 234

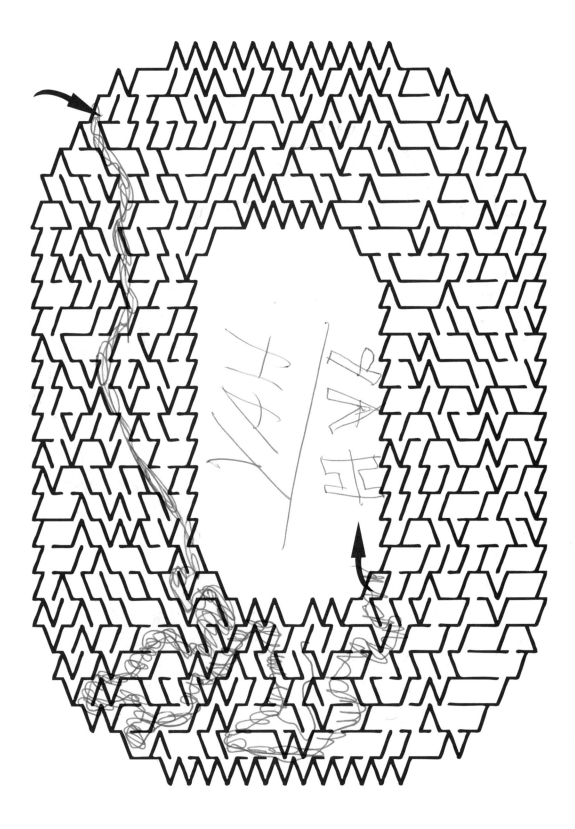

Oval 2

Solution on page 234

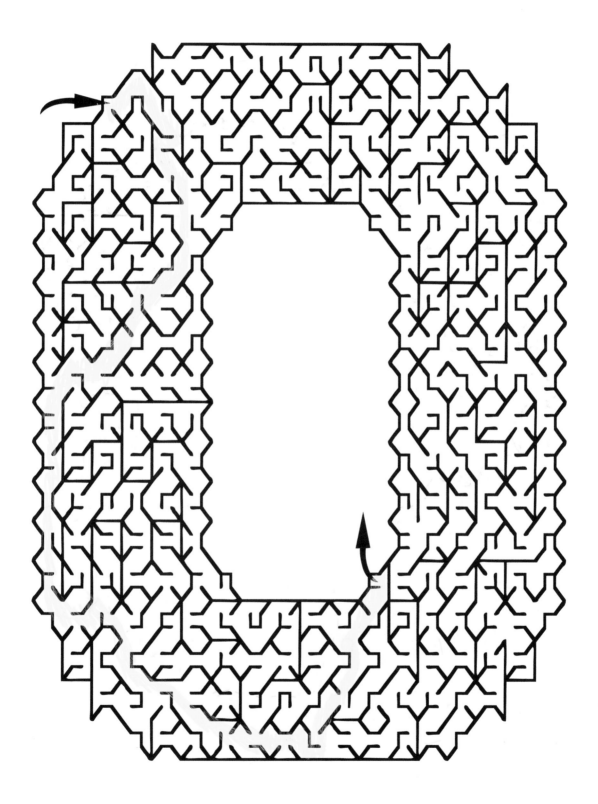

Figure Eight 1

Solution on page 235

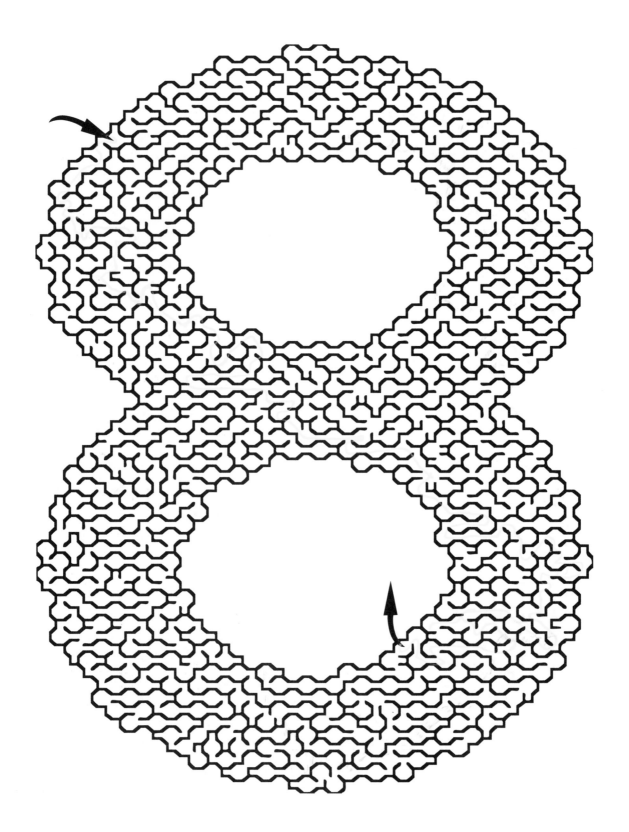

Figure Eight 2

Solution on page 235

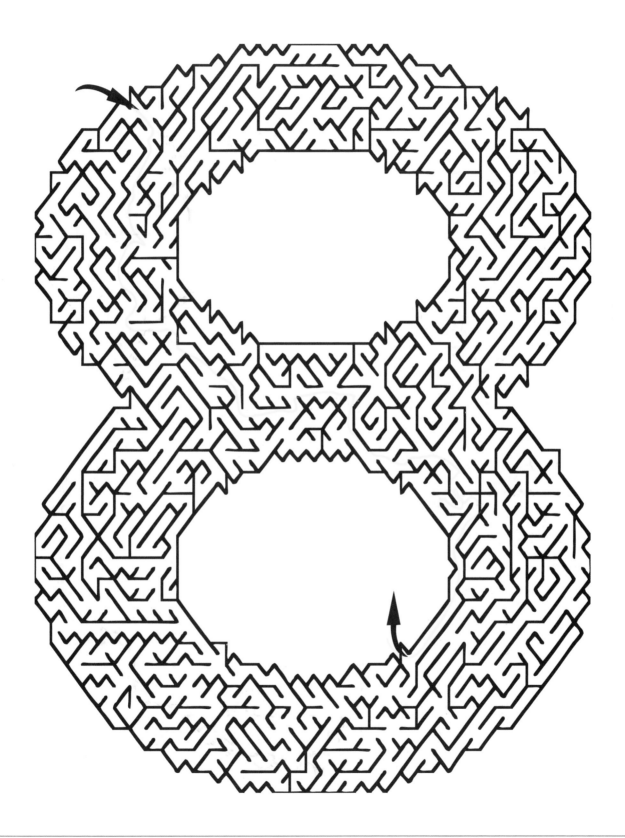

Texas

Solution on page 235

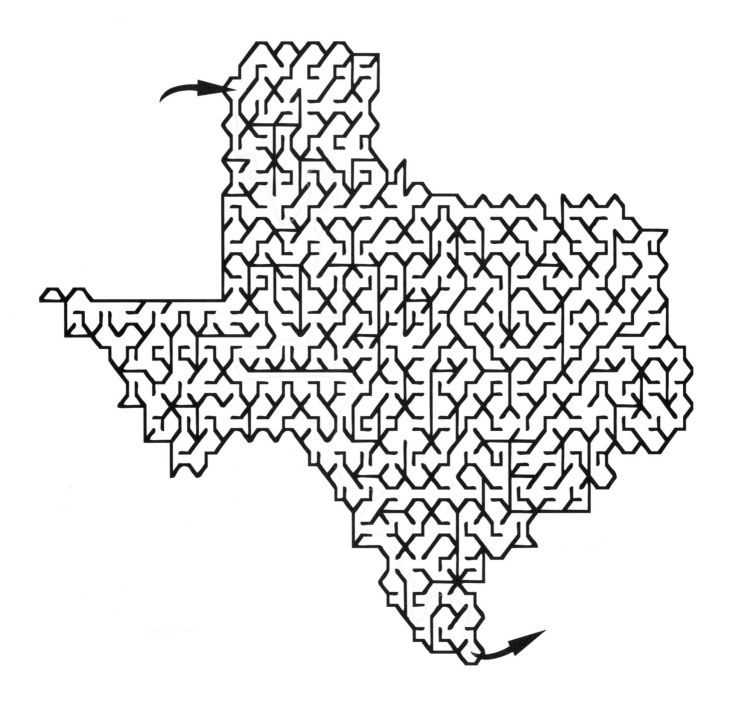

New York

Solution on page 235

California

Solution on page 236

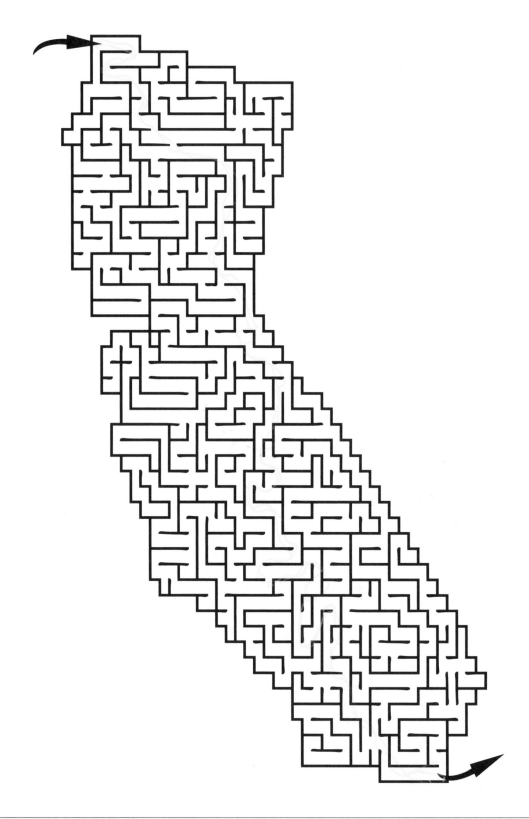

Idaho

Solution on page 236

Indiana

Solution on page 236

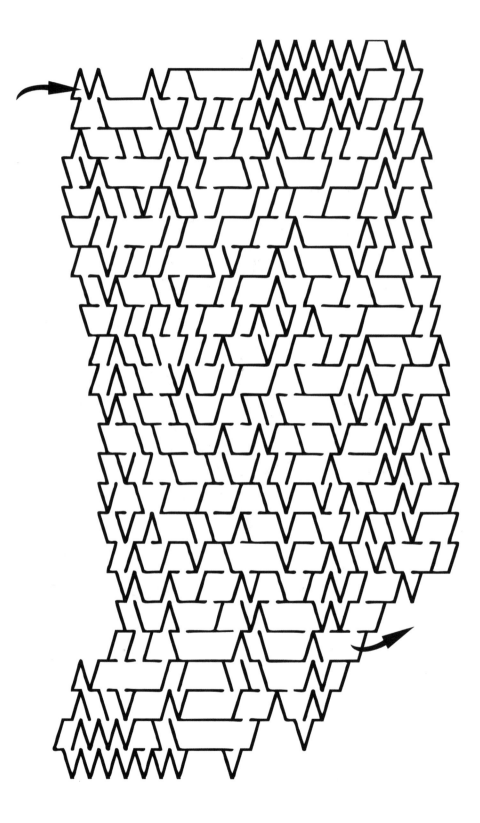

Maine

Solution on page 236

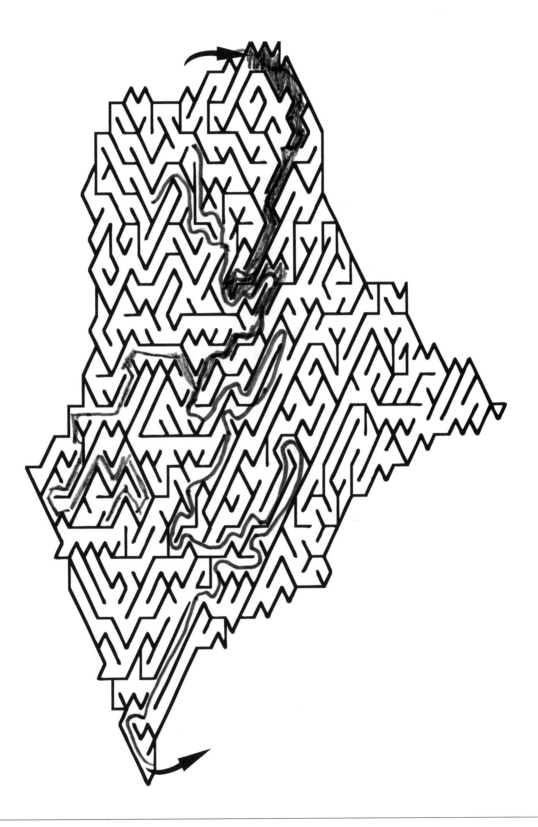

Massachusetts

Solution on page 237

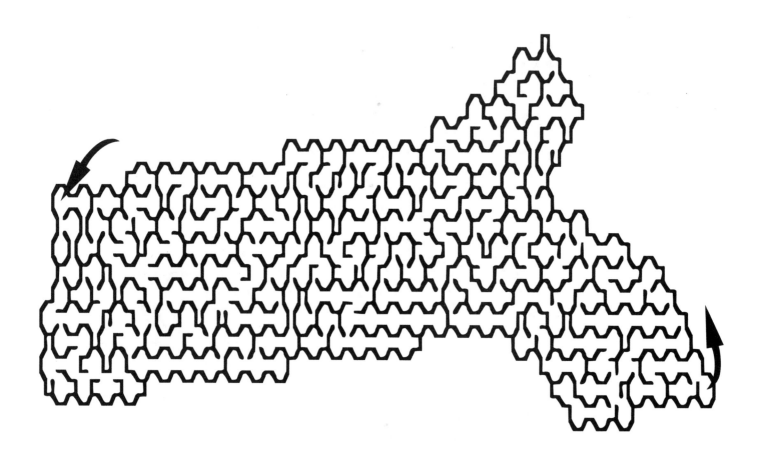

Florida

Solution on page 237

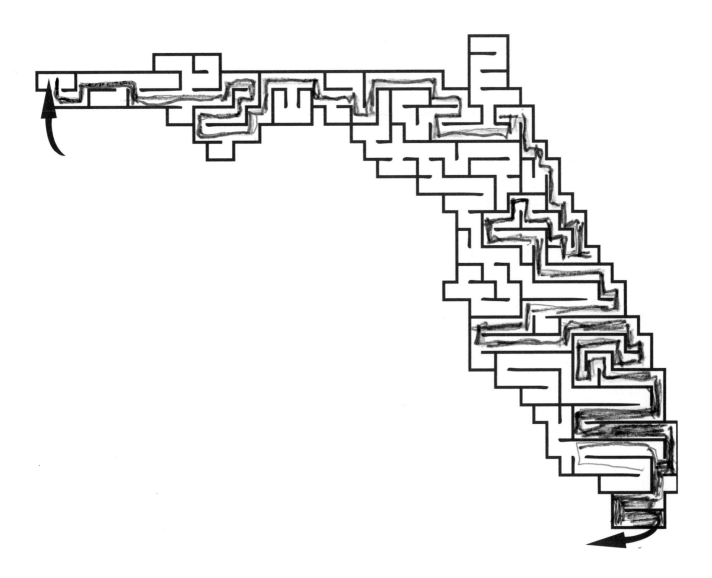

Nevada

Solution on page 237

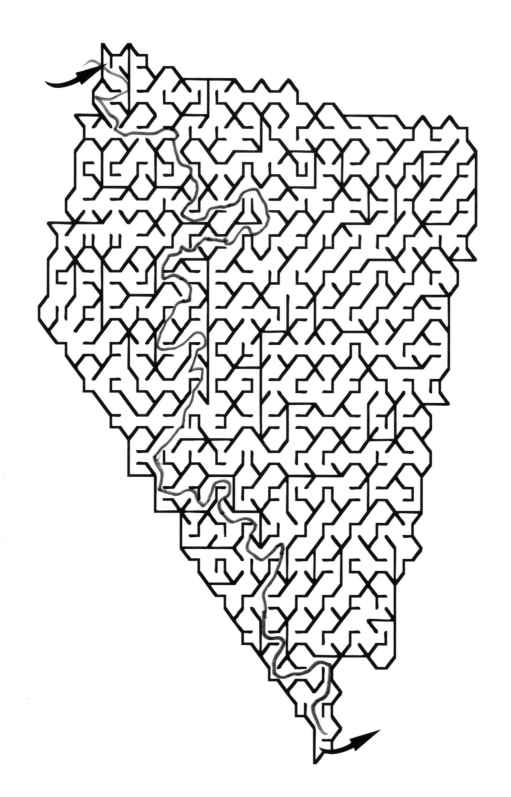

Oklahoma

Solution on page 237

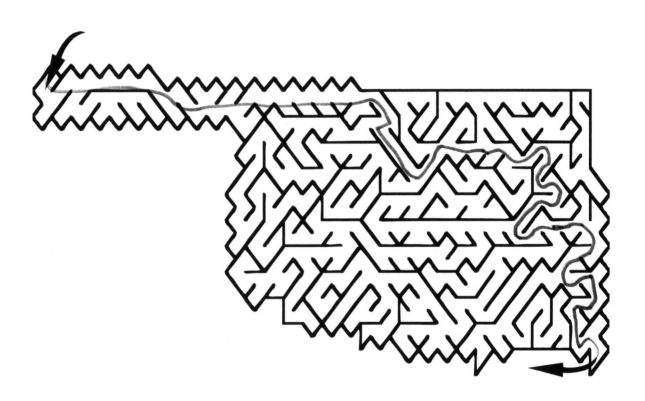

Washington

Solution on page 238

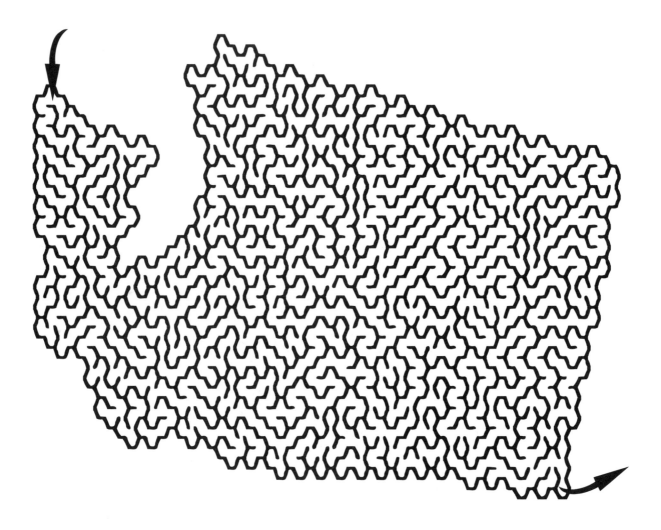

Letter A

Solution on page 238

Letter X

Solution on page 238

Letter P

Solution on page 239

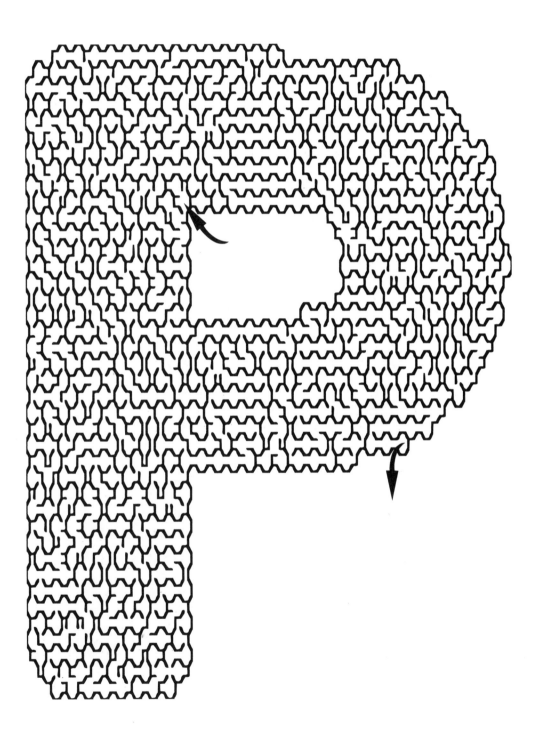

Letter R

Solution on page 239

Letter D

Solution on page 239

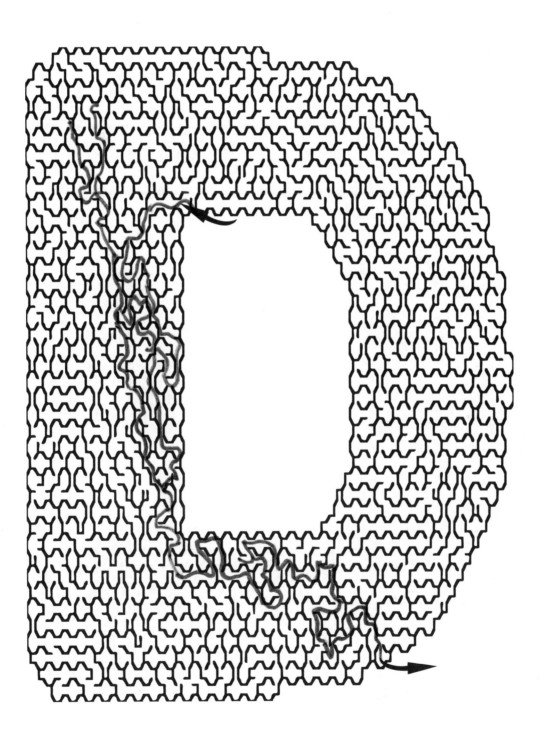

Letter E

Solution on page 239

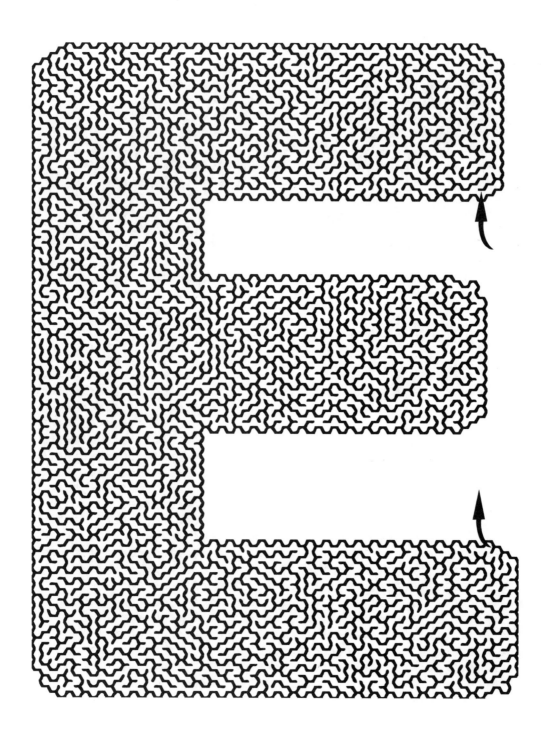

Letter H

Solution on page 240

Letter C

Solution on page 240

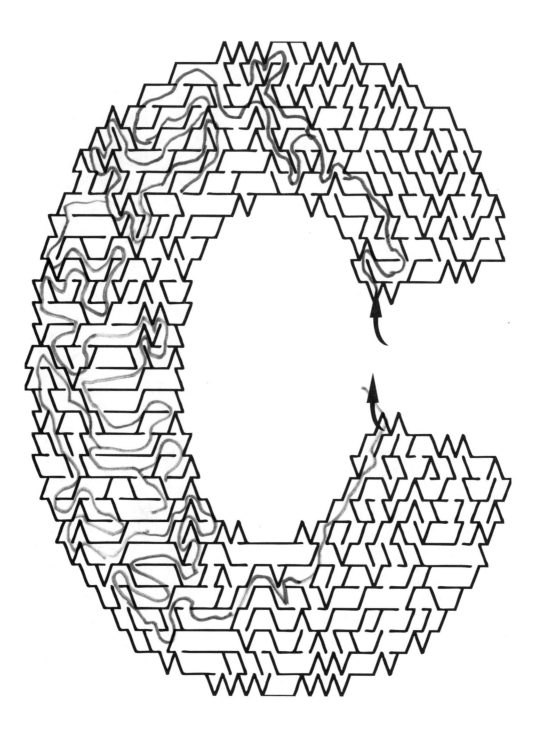

Letter J

Solution on page 240

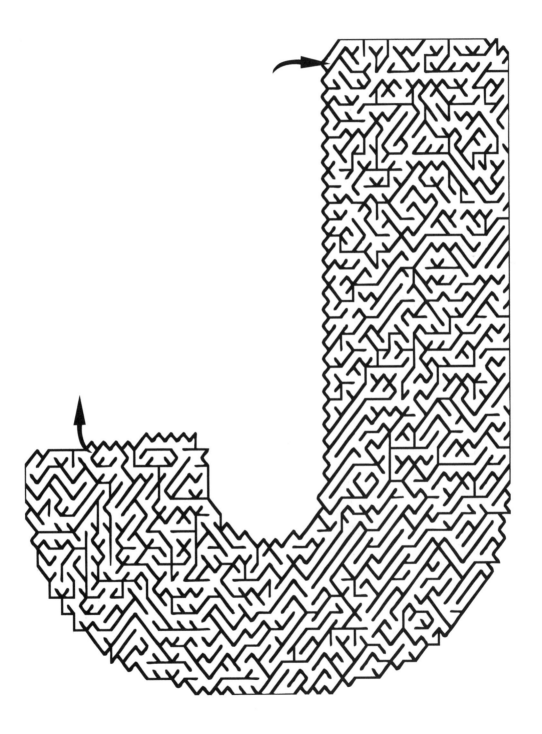

Letter M

Solution on page 240

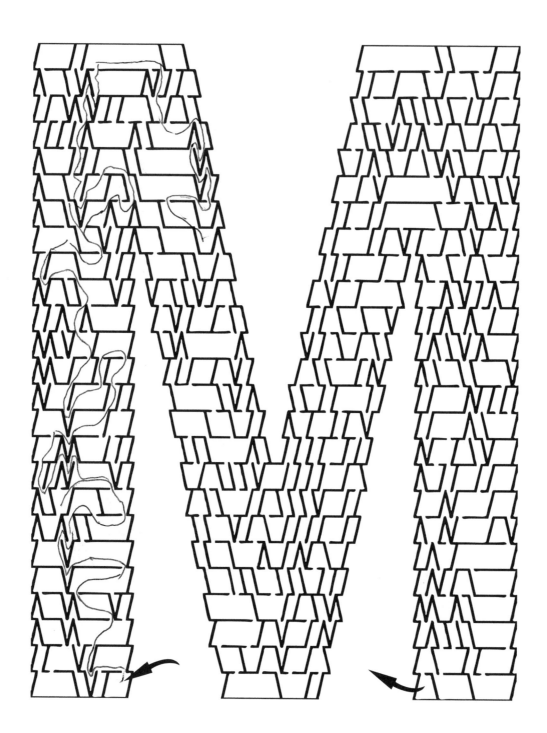

Letter Q

Solution on page 241

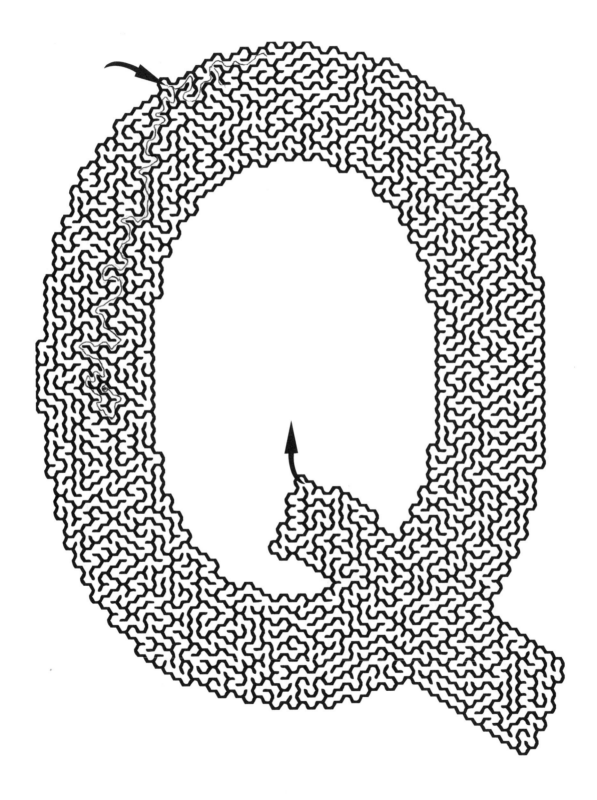

Letter Z

Solution on page 241

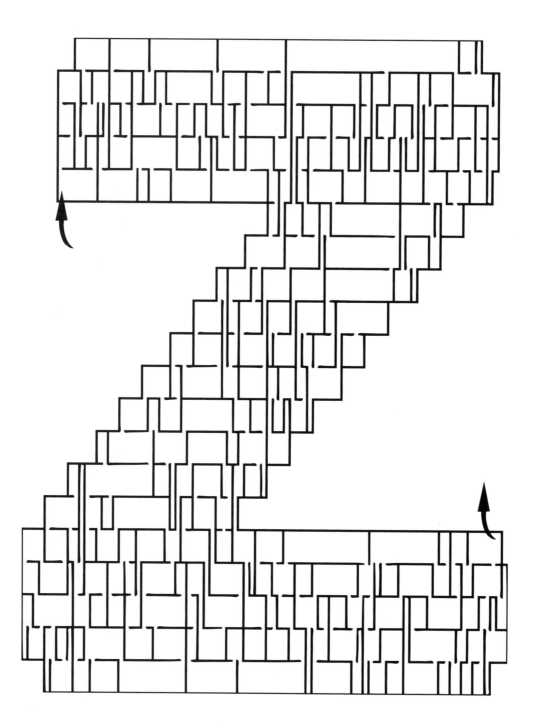

Full Square

Solution on page 241

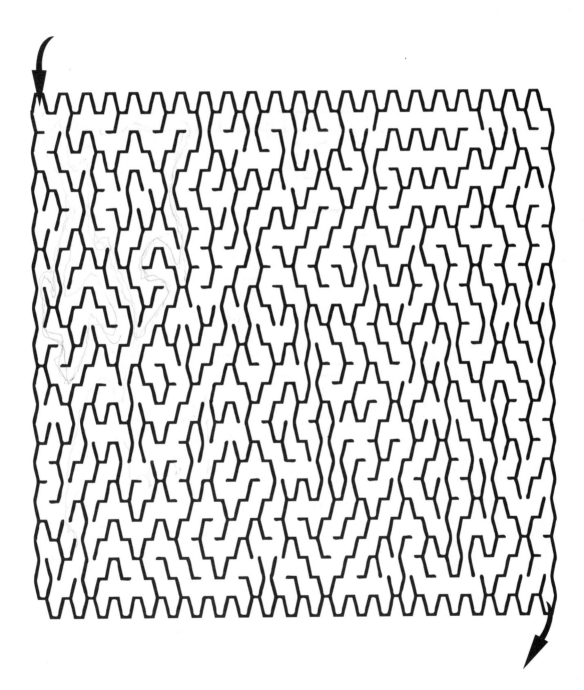

Four Sides

Solution on page 241

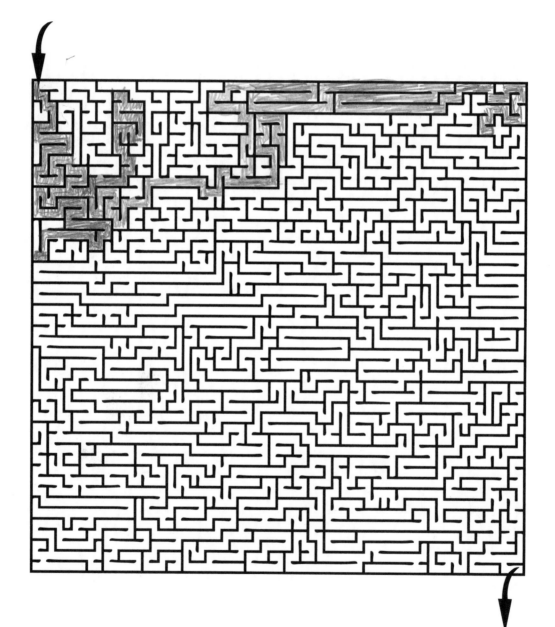

Quadrilateral

Solution on page 242

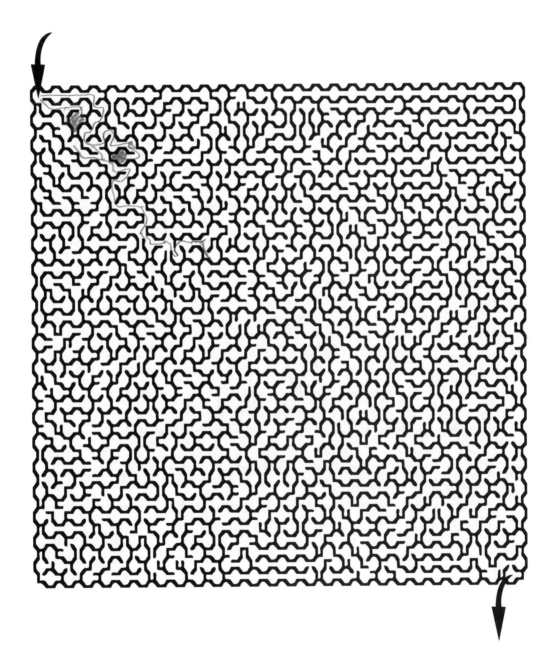

Monolith

Solution on page 242

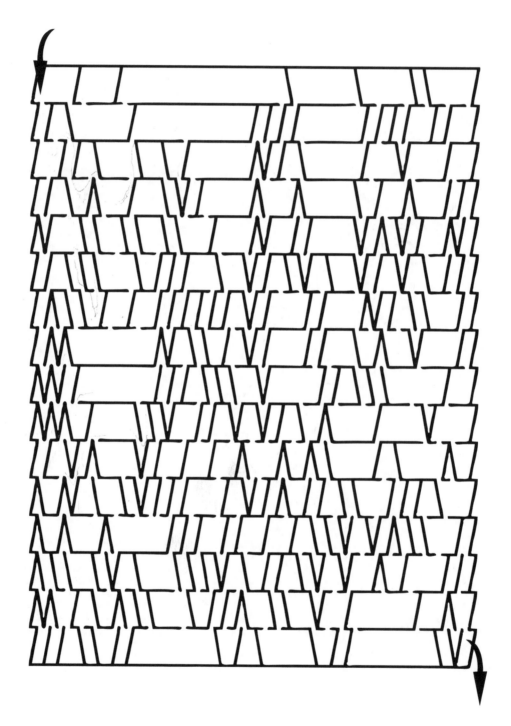

Tall Square

Solution on page 242

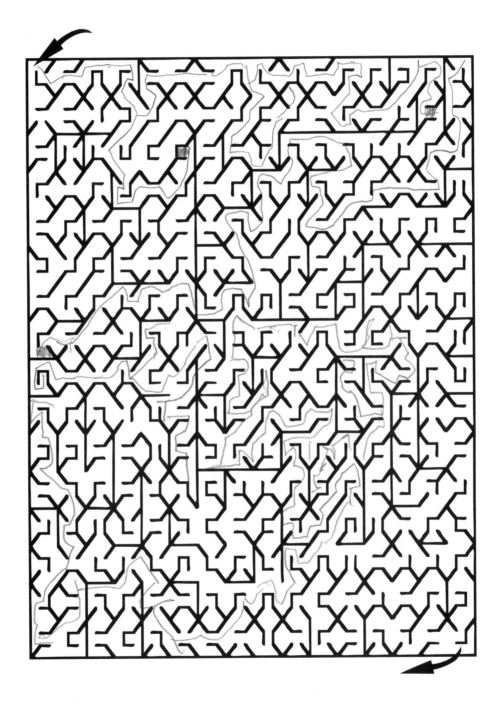

Checkered

Solution on page 242

Framed

Solution on page 243

Square Flower

Solution on page 243

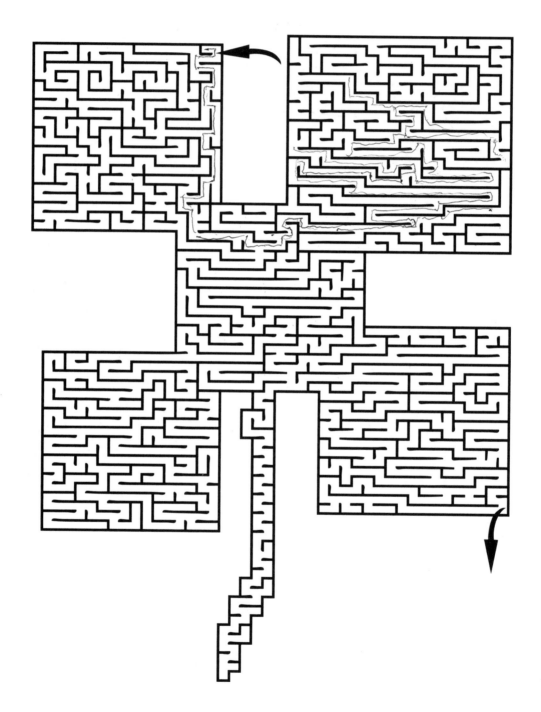

Triple Square

Solution on page 243

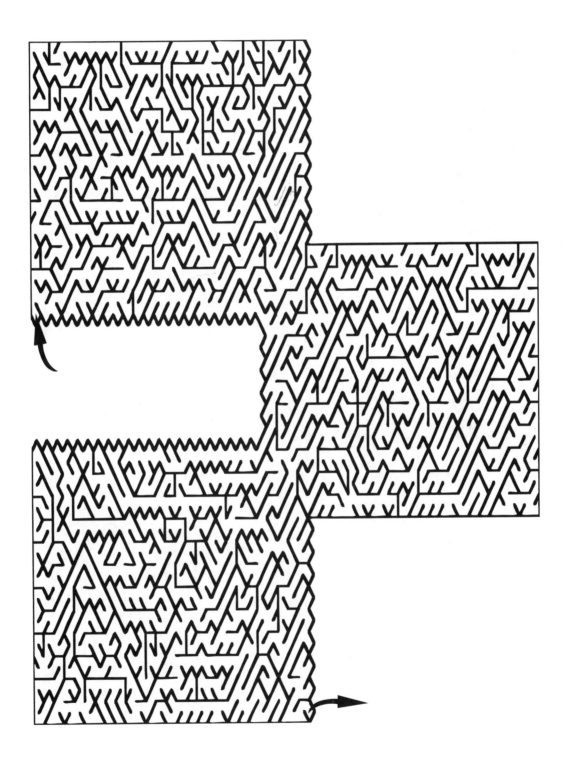

Connected Squares

Solution on page 243

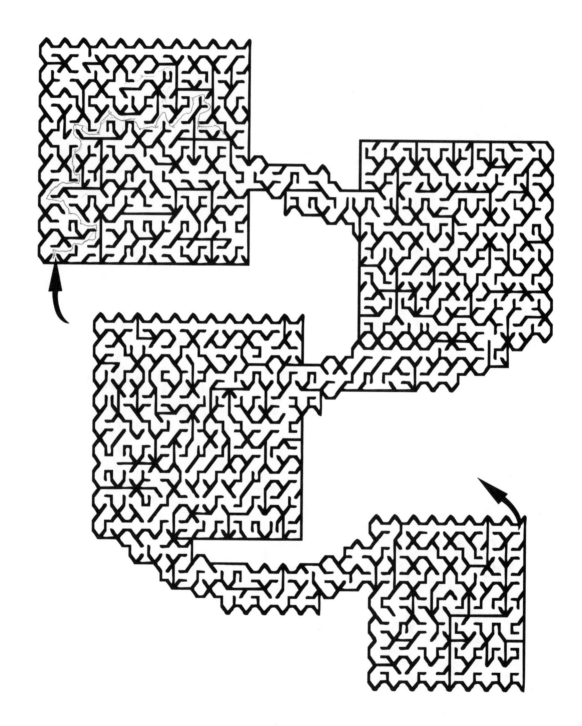

Networked Squares

Solution on page 244

Be My Valentine

Solution on page 244

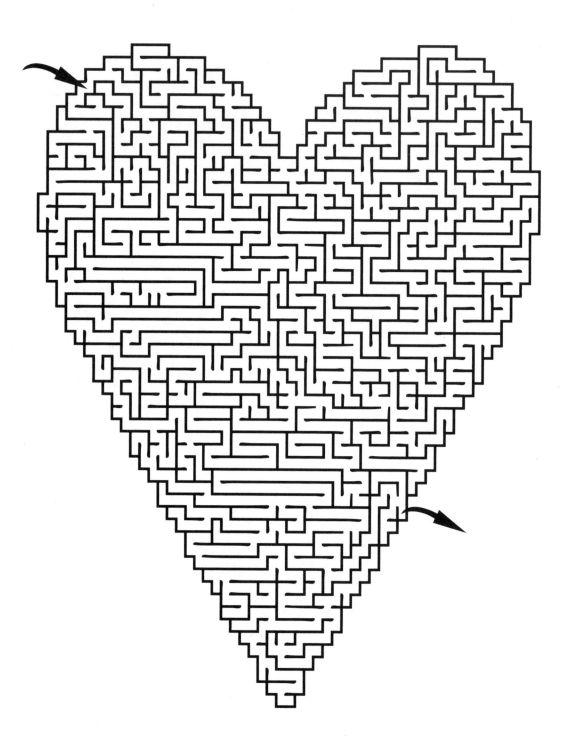

Saint Patrick's Day Shamrock

Solution on page 244

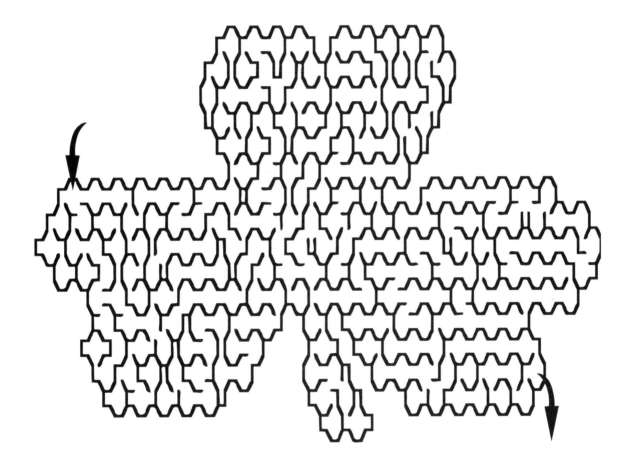

Easter Egg

Solution on page 245

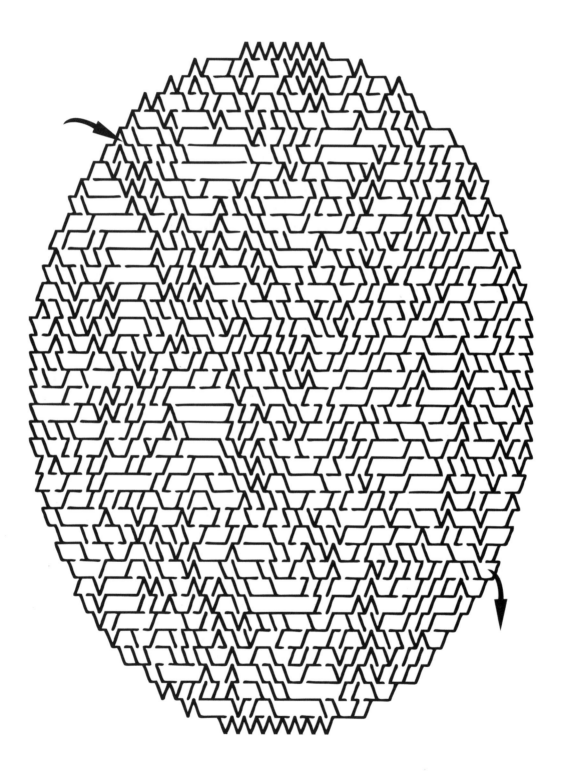

Easter Bunny

Solution on page 245

Halloween Ghost

Solution on page 245

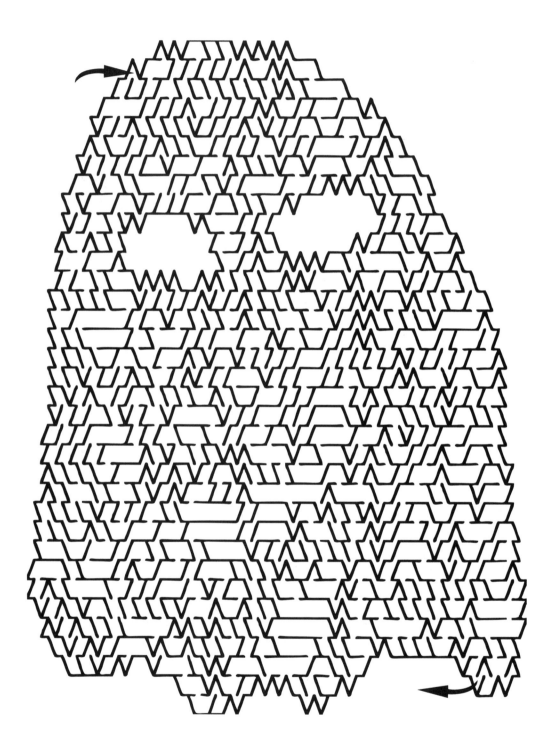

Jack-O'-Lantern

Solution on page 245

Halloween Bat

Solution on page 246

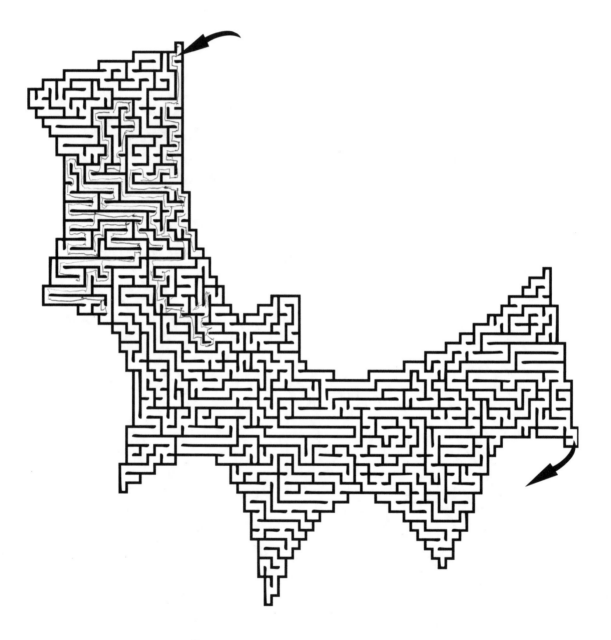

Dreidel

Solution on page 246

Christmas Ornaments

Solution on page 246

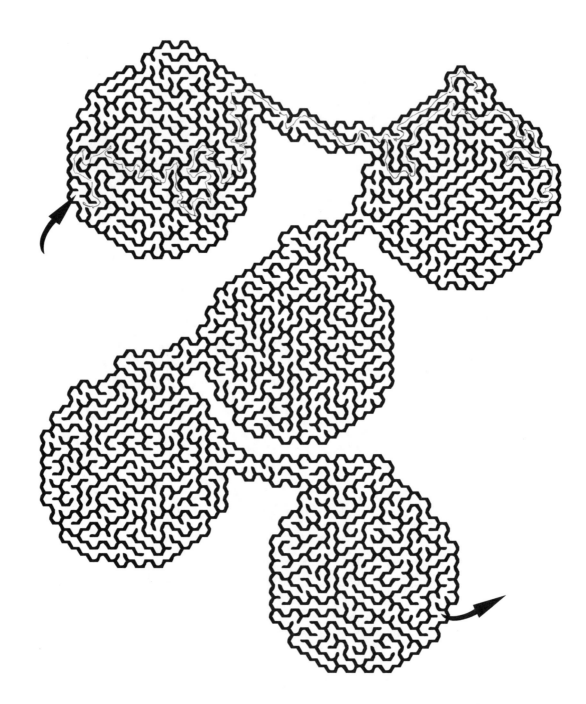

Candy Cane

Solution on page 246

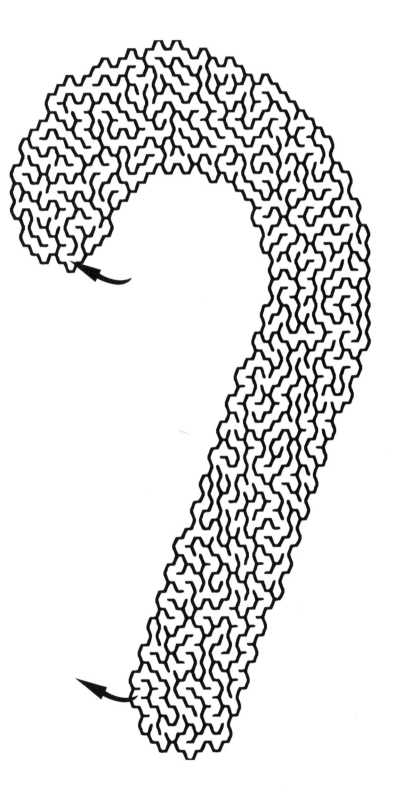

Christmas Tree

Solution on page 247

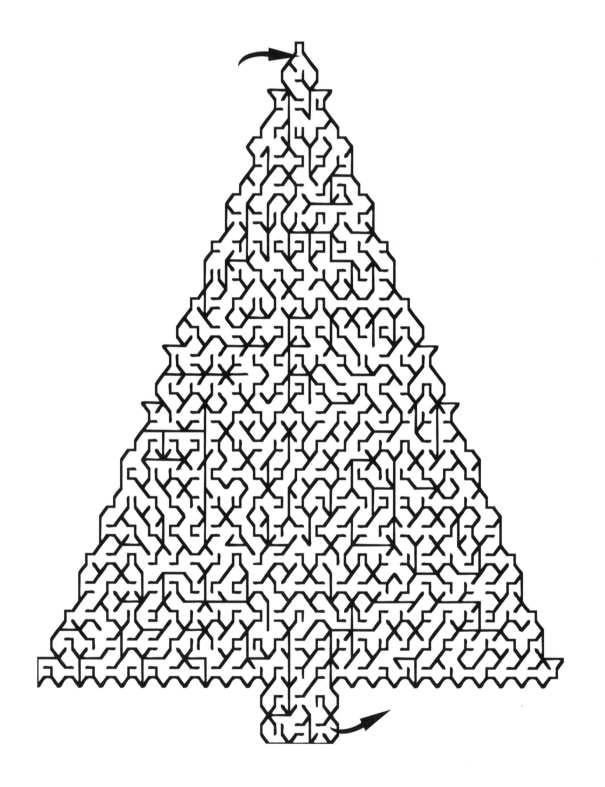

Chapter 7: Mazes Take Off!

Space Pod

Solution on page 247

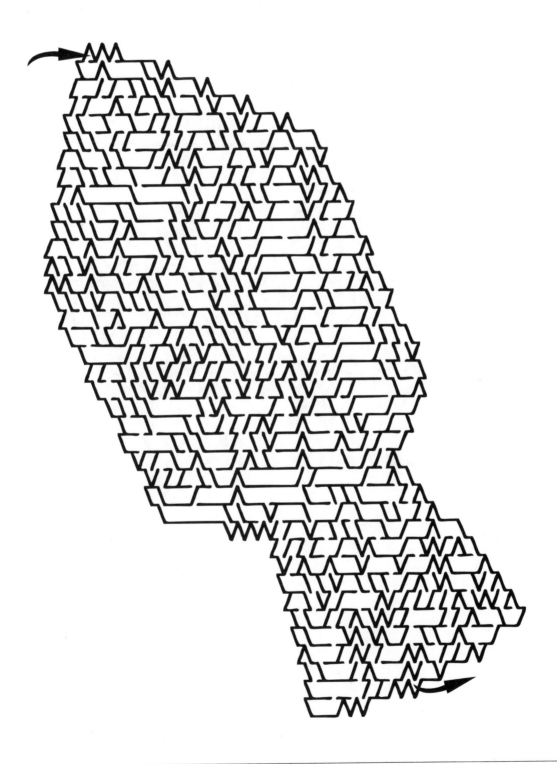

UFO

Solution on page 247

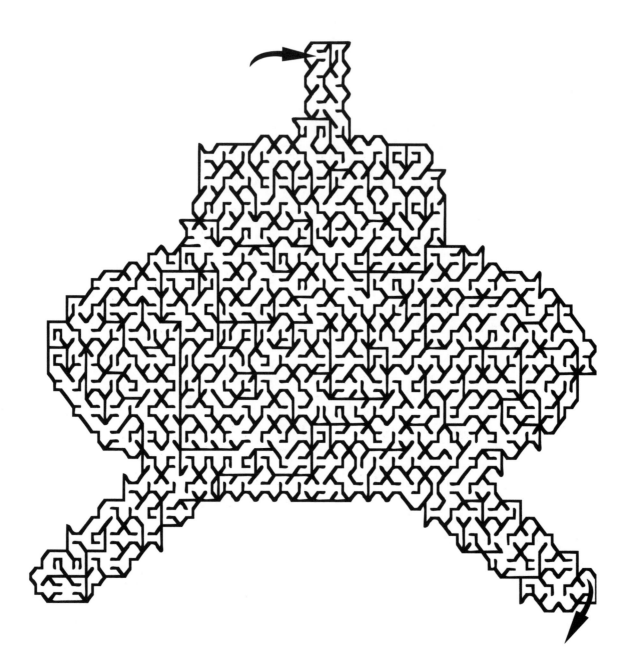

Splashdown Capsule

Solution on page 248

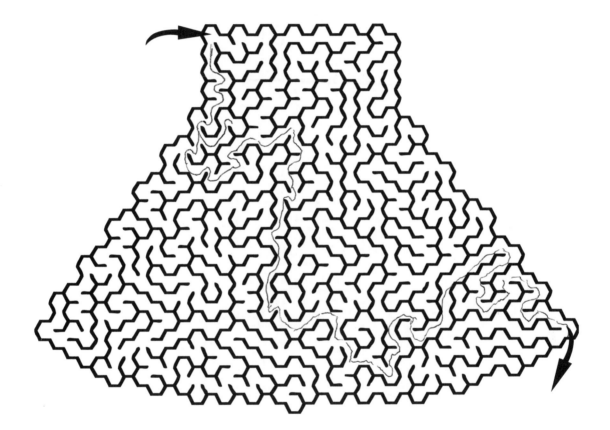

Apollo

Solution on page 248

Martian Invader

Solution on page 248

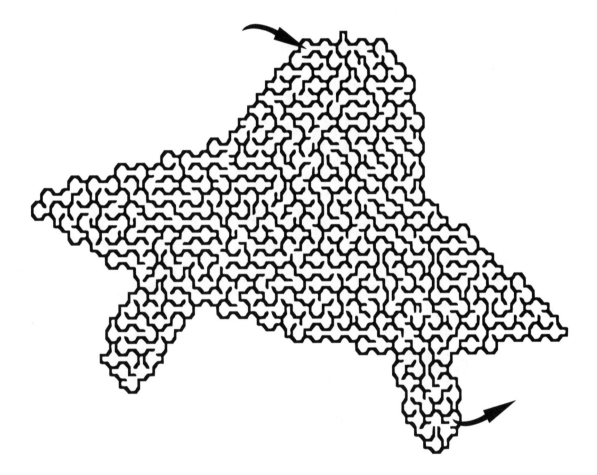

Lunar Lander

Solution on page 248

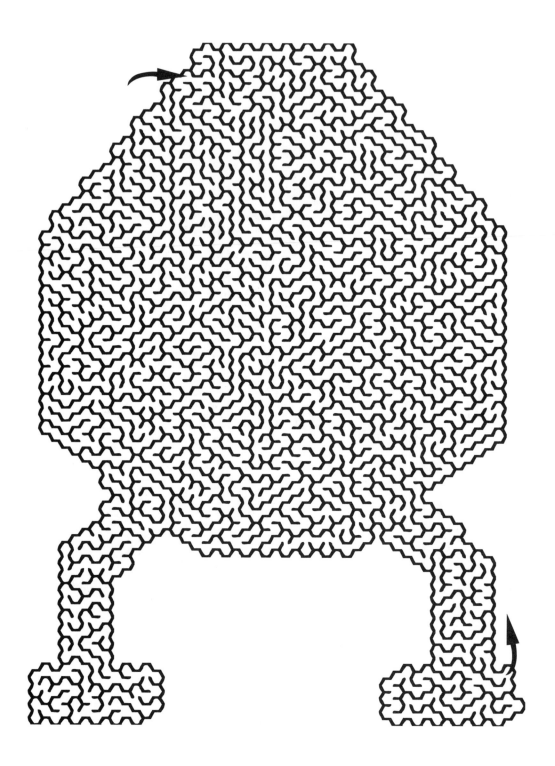

Space Shuttle

Solution on page 249

Lighthouse

Solution on page 249

City Homes

Solution on page 249

Barn

Solution on page 250

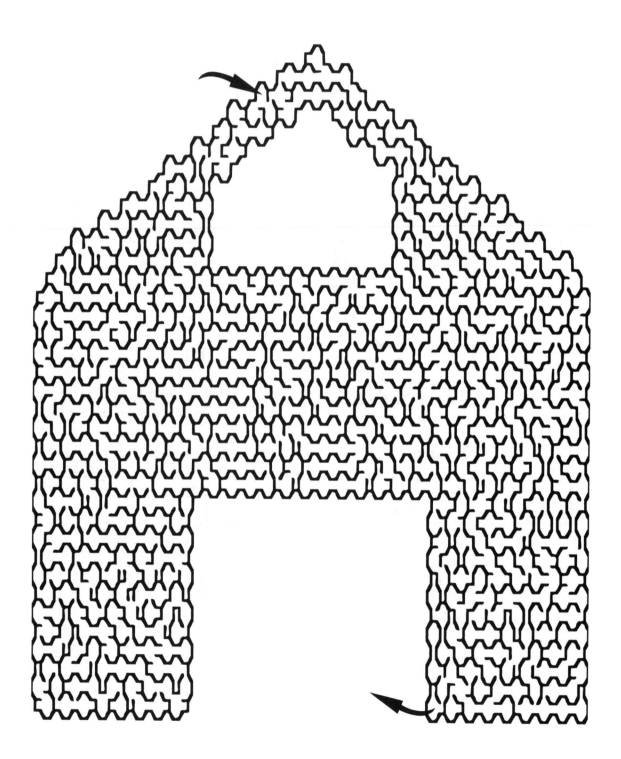

Igloo

Solution on page 250

Doghouse

Solution on page 250

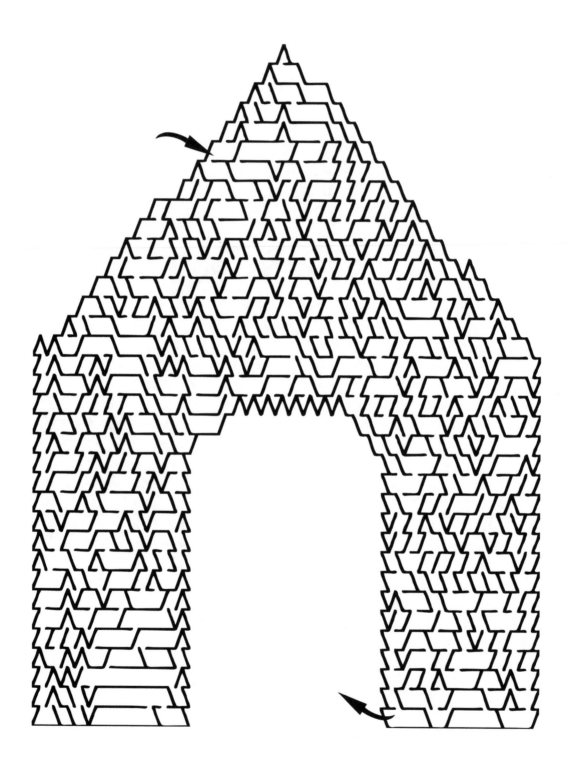

Teepee

Solution on page 250

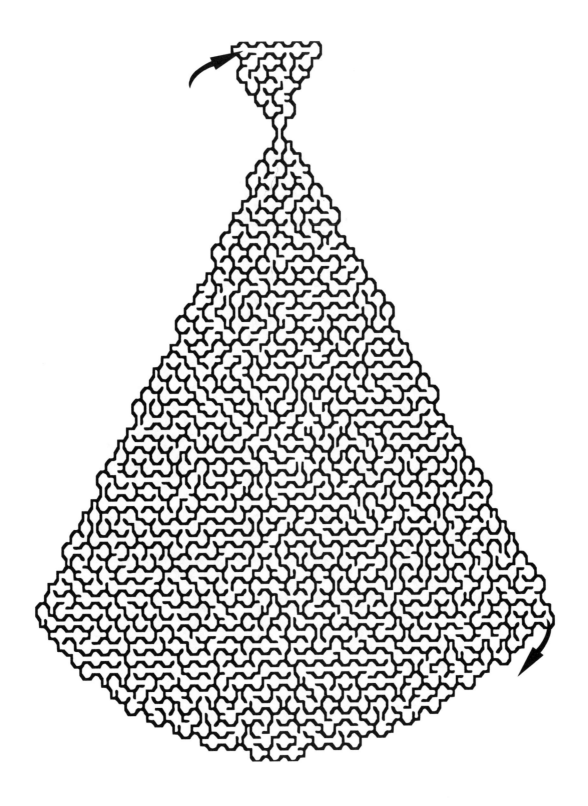

Birdhouse

Solution on page 251

Hut

Solution on page 251

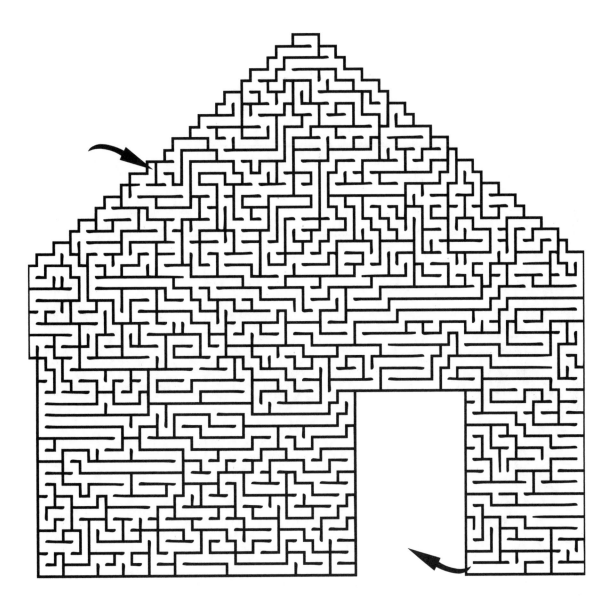

Townhouse

Solution on page 251

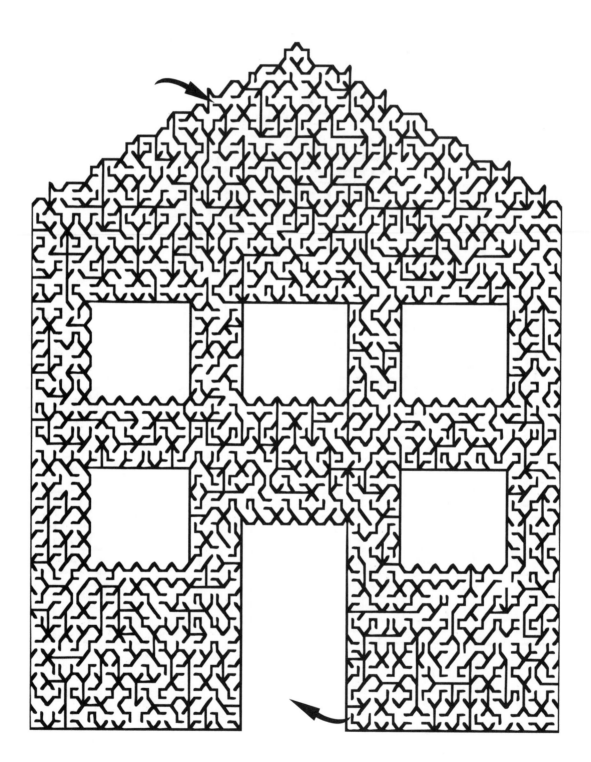

A-Frame

Solution on page 251

Cheerful

Solution on page 252

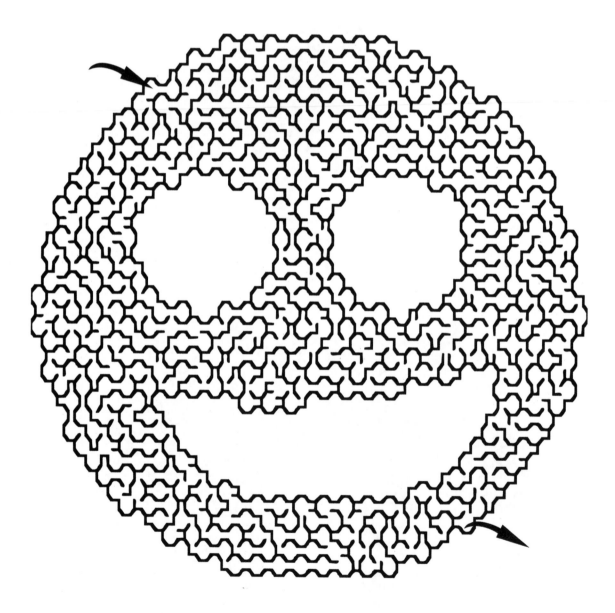

Big Laugh

Solution on page 252

Toothy

Solution on page 252

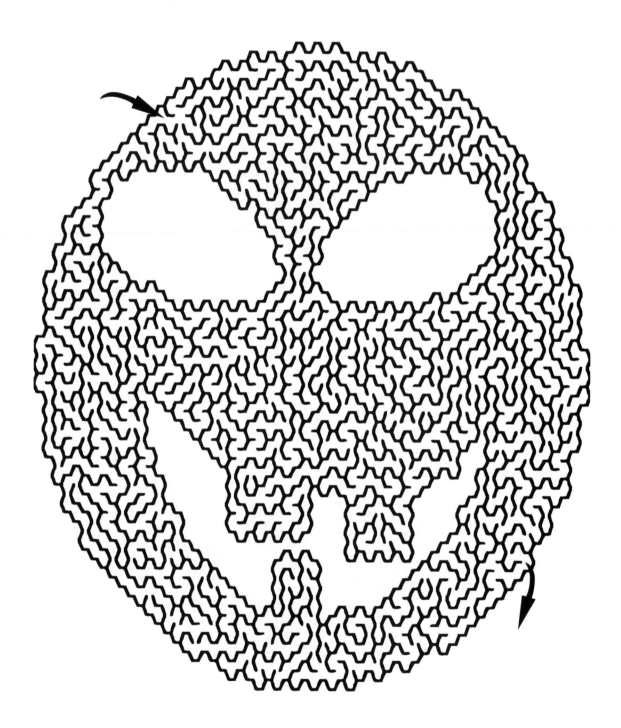

Smile

Solution on page 252

Friendly

Solution on page 253

Sinister

Solution on page 253

Egghead

Solution on page 253

Pleased

Solution on page 253

Singer

Solution on page 254

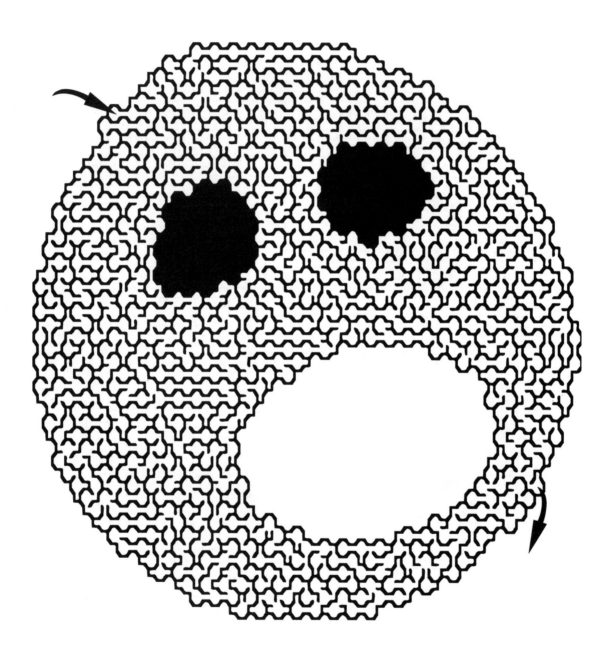

Zero

Solution on page 254

One

Solution on page 254

Two

Solution on page 255

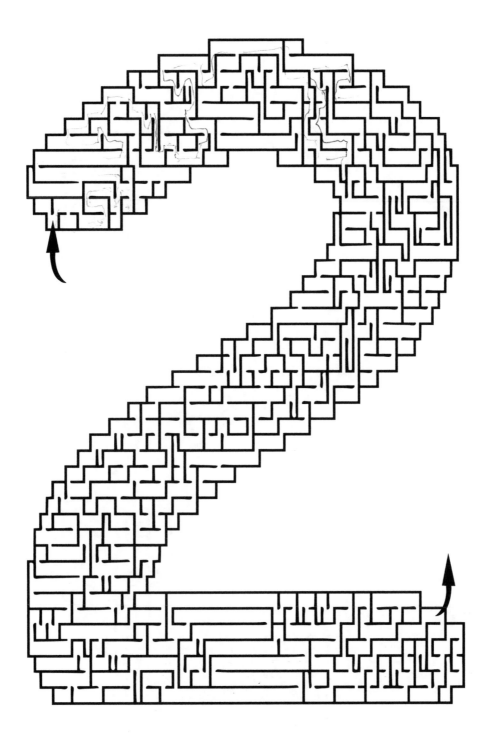

Three

Solution on page 255

Four

Solution on page 255

Five

Solution on page 255

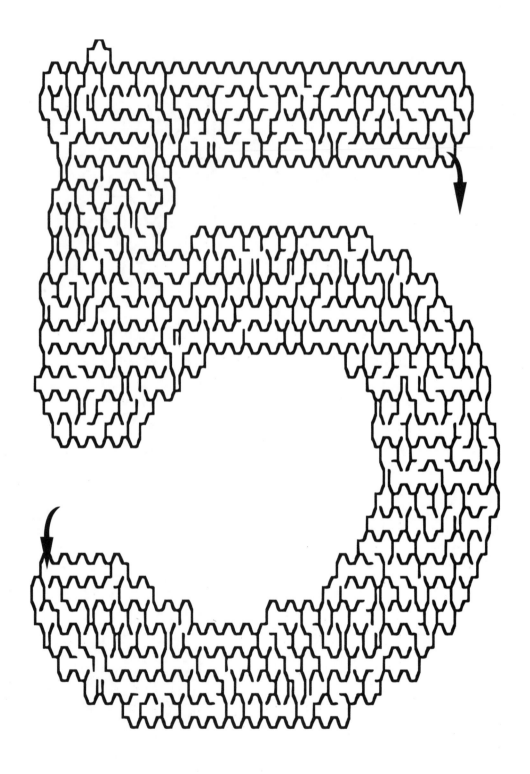

Six

Solution on page 256

Seven

Solution on page 256

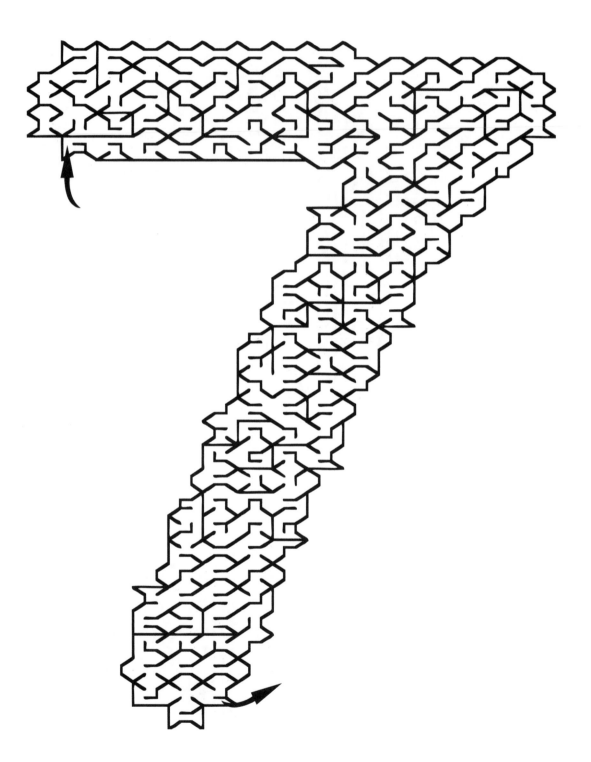

Eight

Solution on page 256

Nine

Solution on page 256

Twenty-One

Solution on page 257

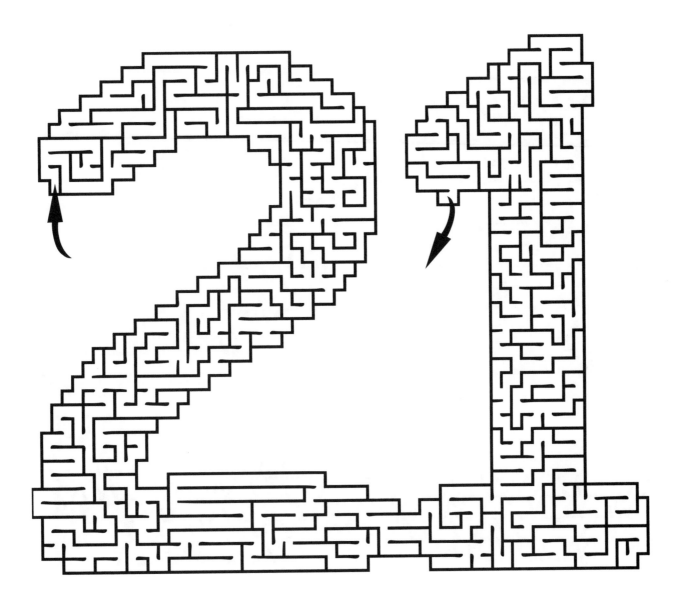

Fifty-Six

Solution on page 257

Six Points

Solution on page 257

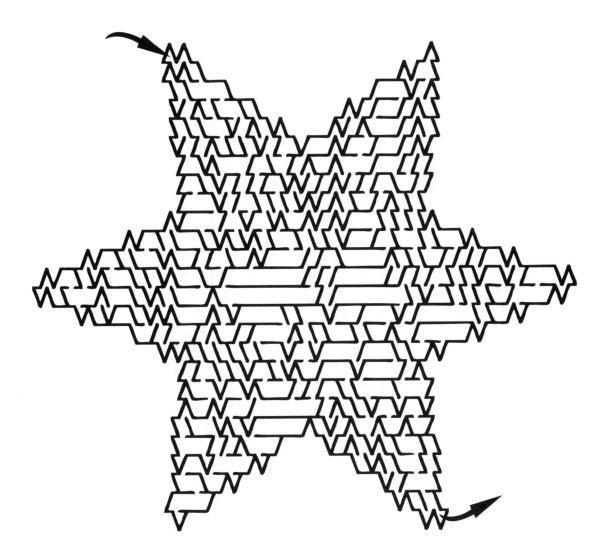

Five Stars

Solution on page 257

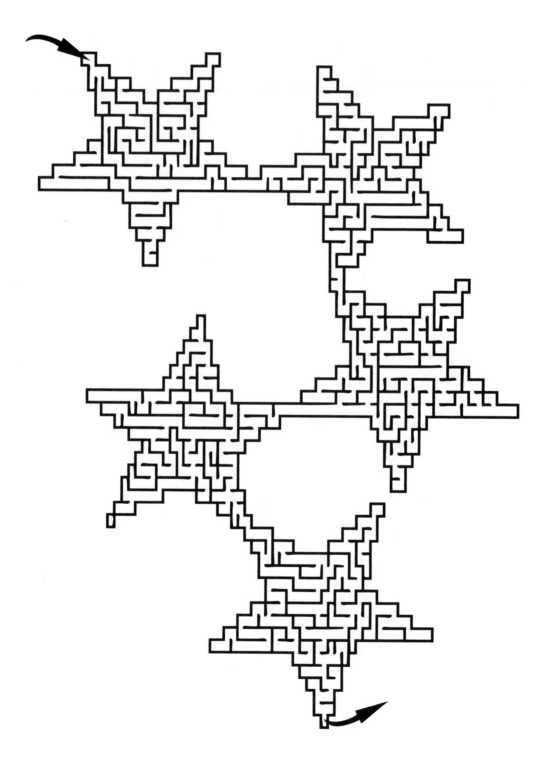

Five Points

Solution on page 258

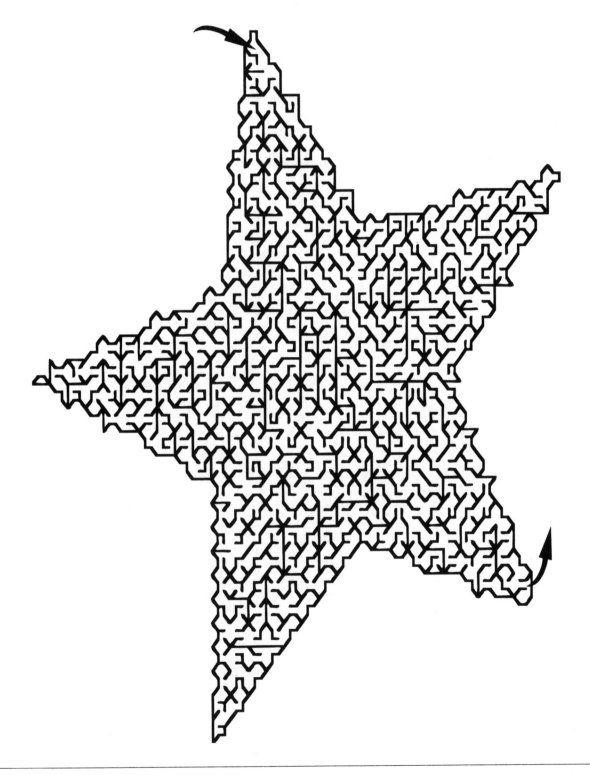

Seven Points

Solution on page 258

Hollow Star

Solution on page 258

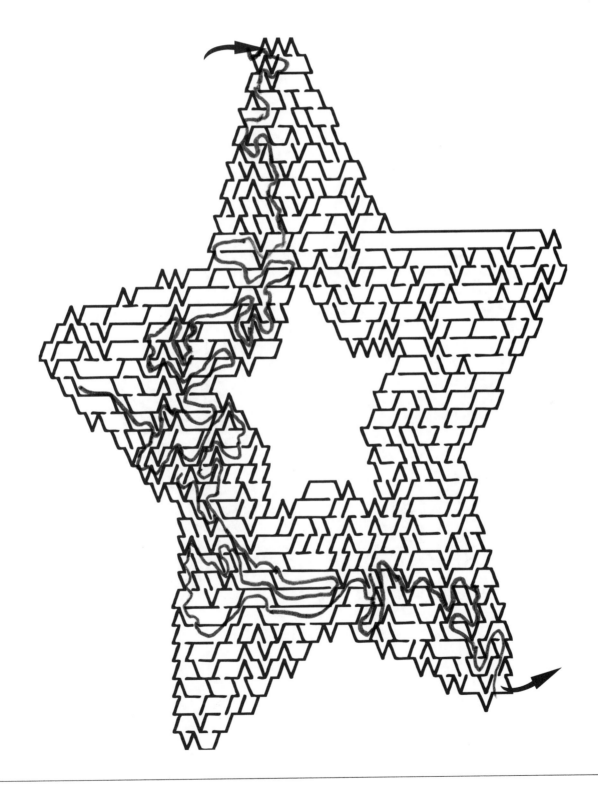

Four Stars

Solution on page 258

Designer Star

Solution on page 259

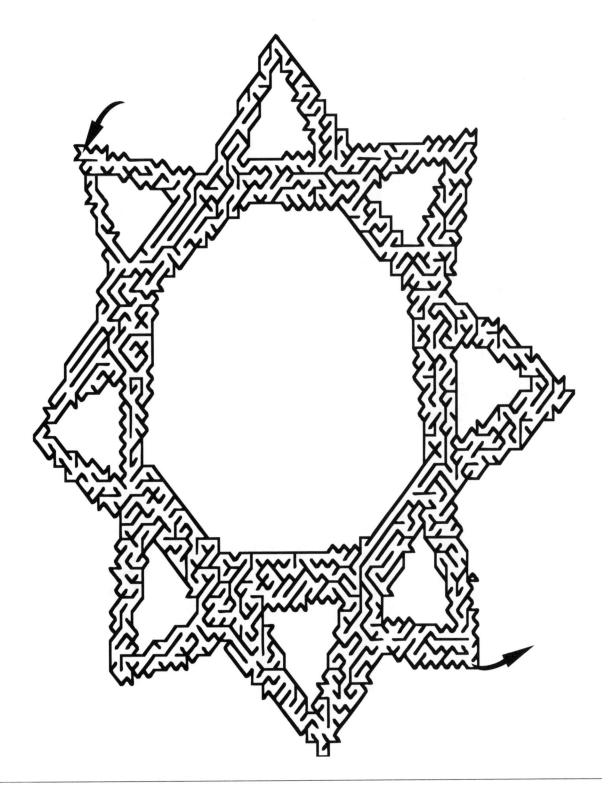

Pointy Star

Solution on page 259

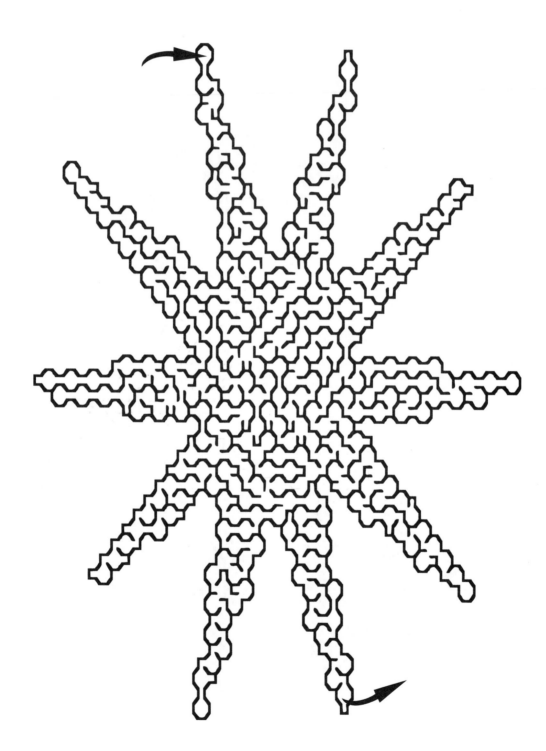

Sea Star

Solution on page 259

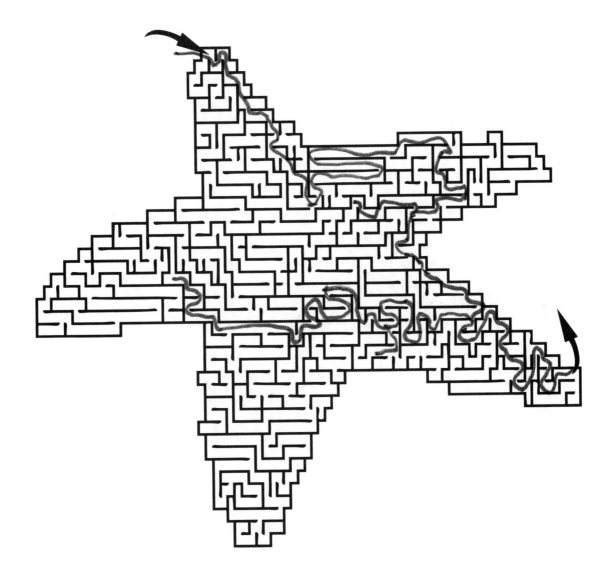

Chapter 12: Butterfly Mazes

Butterfly 1

Solution on page 259

Solution on page 260

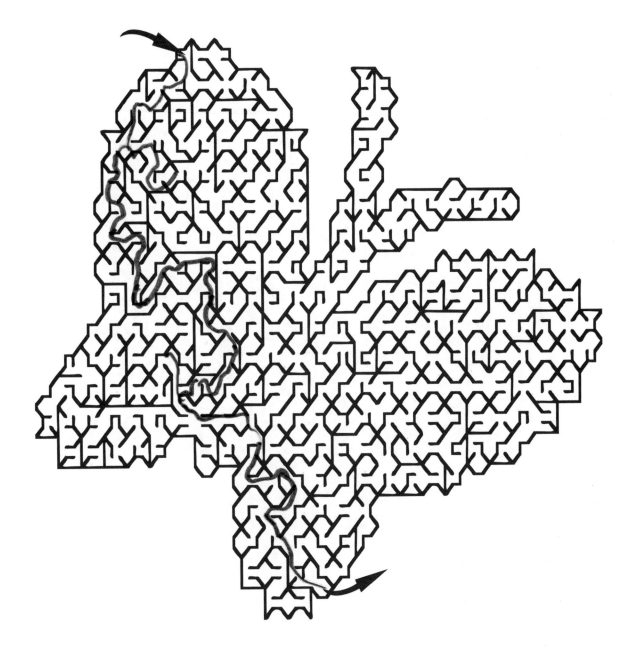

Butterfly 3

Solution on page 260

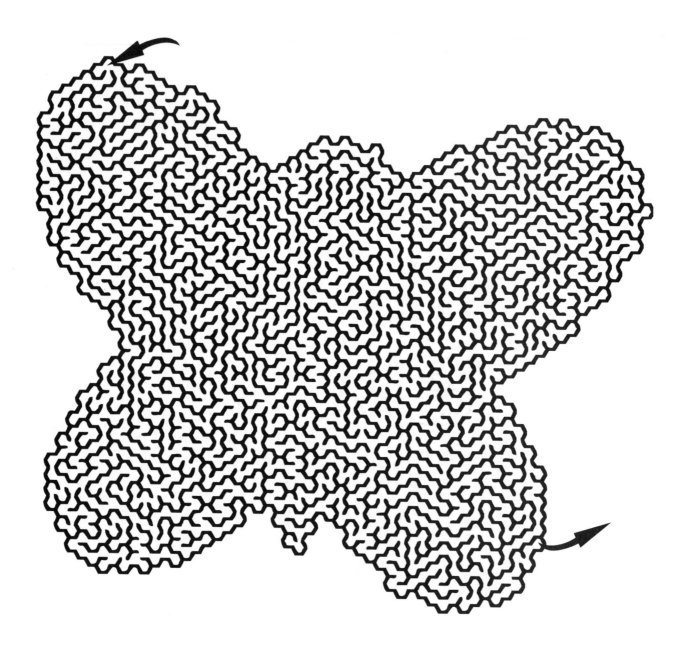

Butterfly 4

Solution on page 260

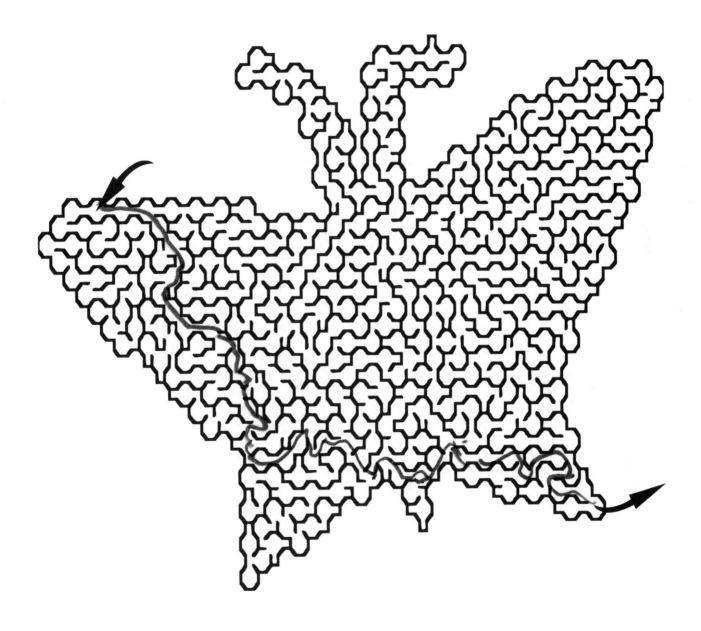

Butterfly 5

Solution on page 260

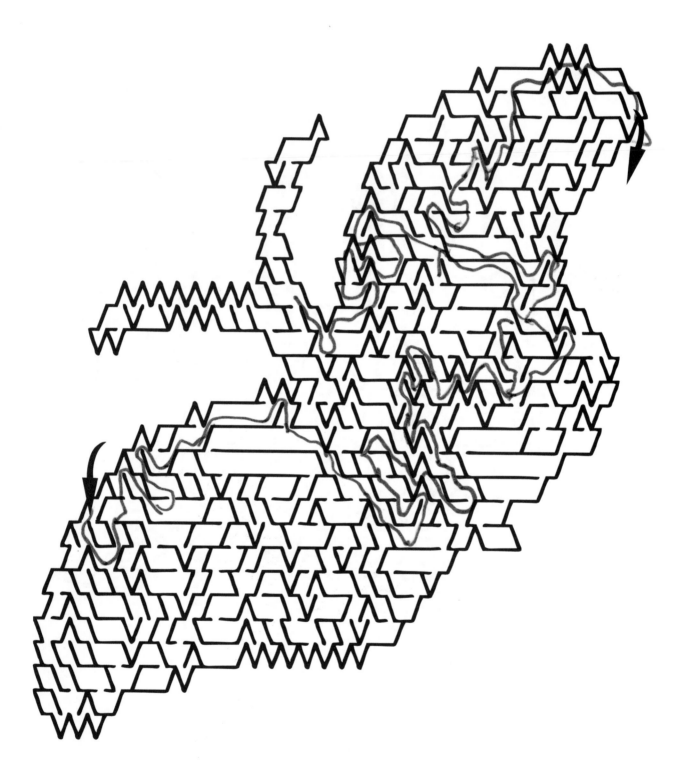

Butterfly 6

Solution on page 261

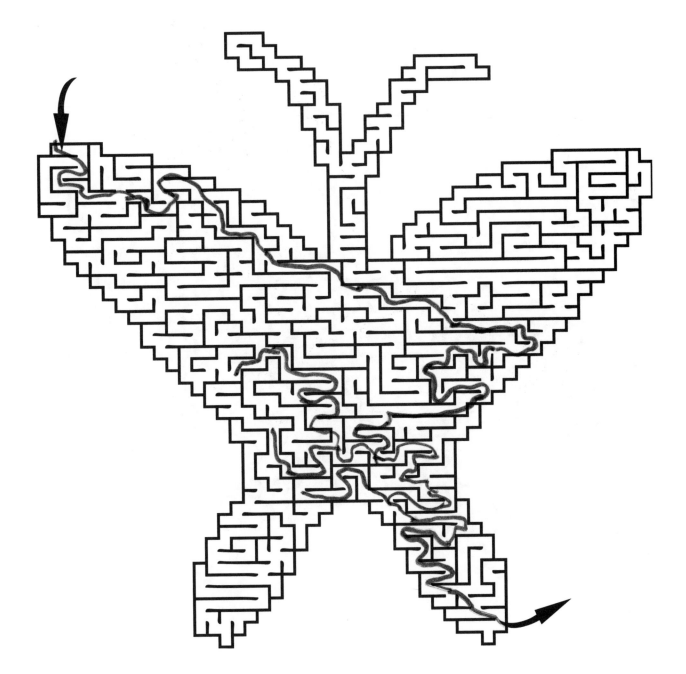

Butterfly 7

Solution on page 261

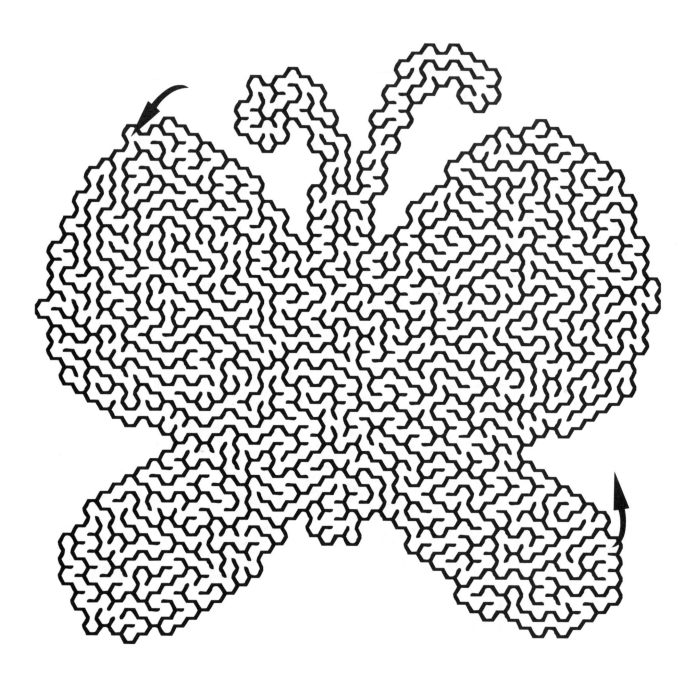

Butterfly 8

Solution on page 261

Butterfly 9

Solution on page 261

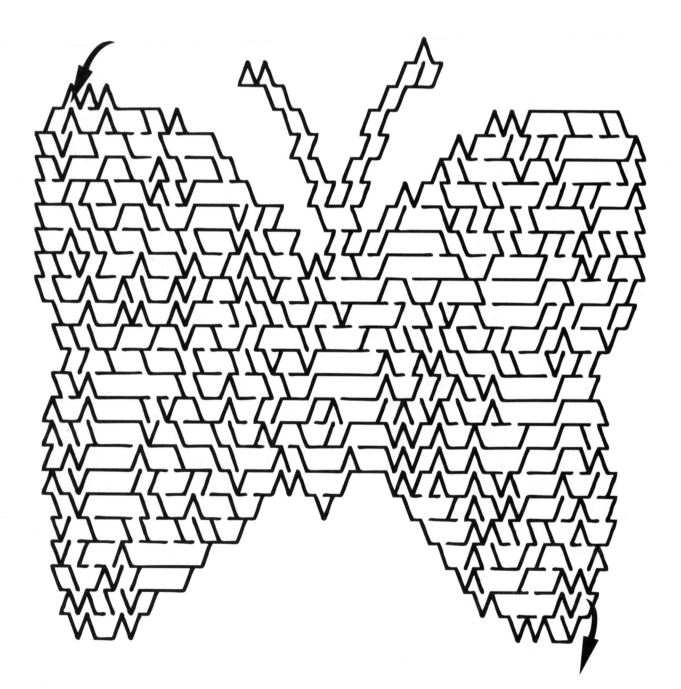

Butterfly 10

Solution on page 262

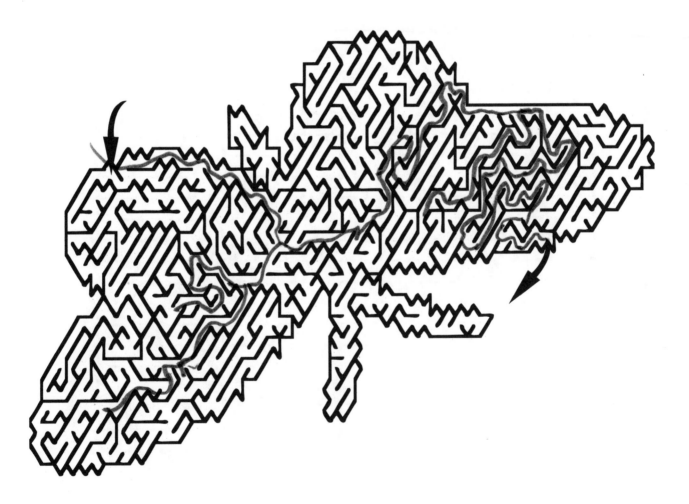

Big Nose

Solution on page 262

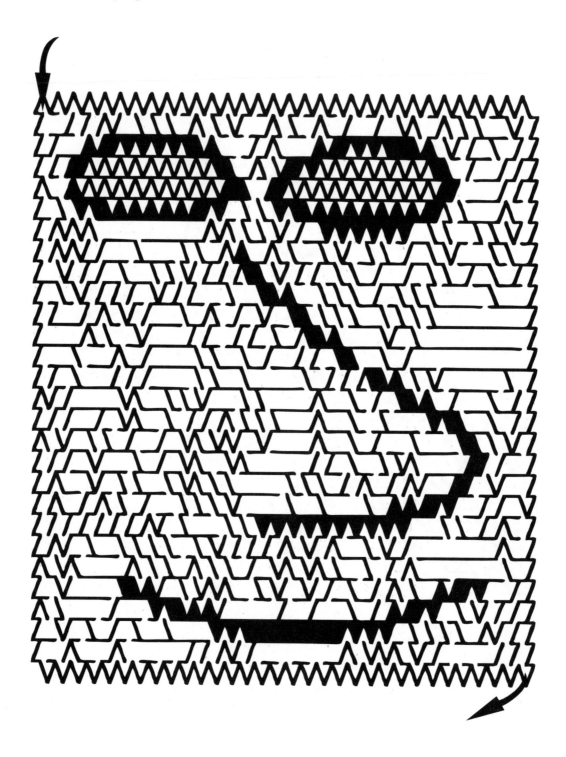

Shades

Solution on page 262

Robot

Solution on page 263

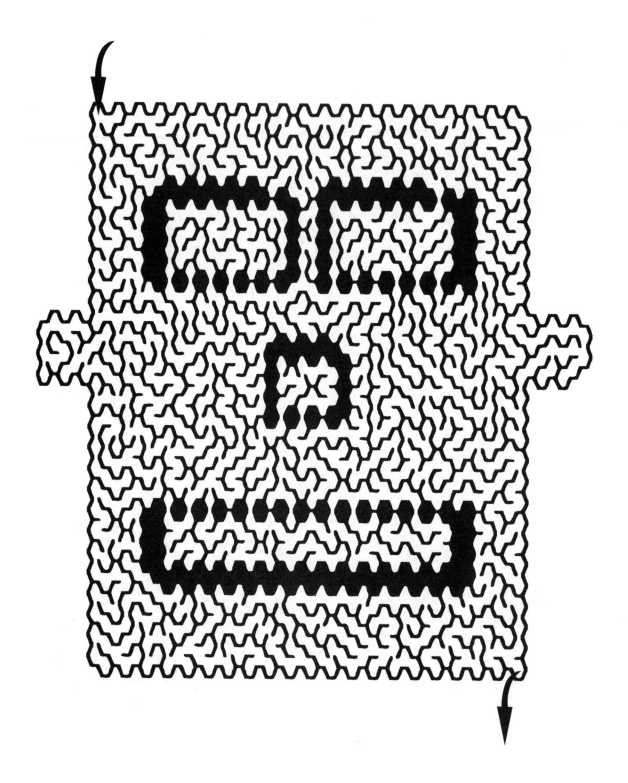

Big Smile

Solution on page 263

Devious

Solution on page 263

Big Mouth

Solution on page 263

Frown

Solution on page 264

Wry

Solution on page 264

Happy

Solution on page 264

Surprised

Solution on page 264

Flower 1

Solution on page 265

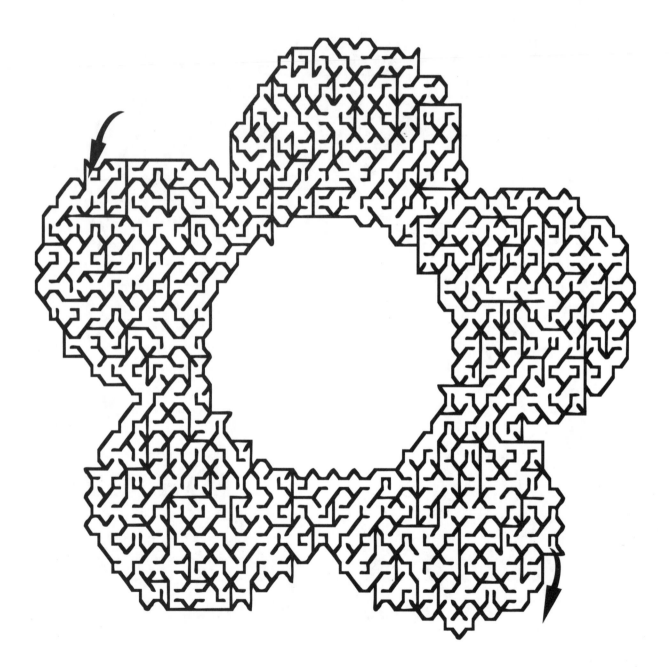

Flower 2

Solution on page 265

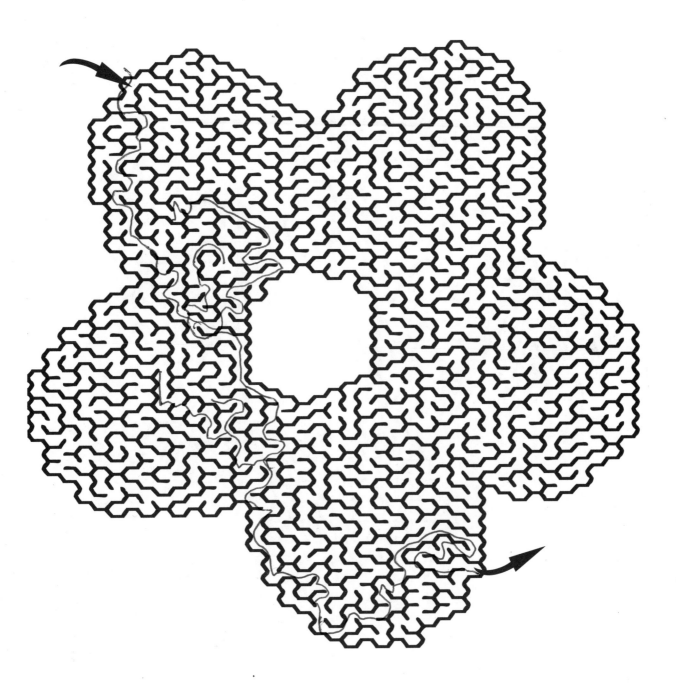

Flower 3

Solution on page 265

Flower 4

Solution on page 265

Flower 5

Solution on page 266

Flower 6

Solution on page 266

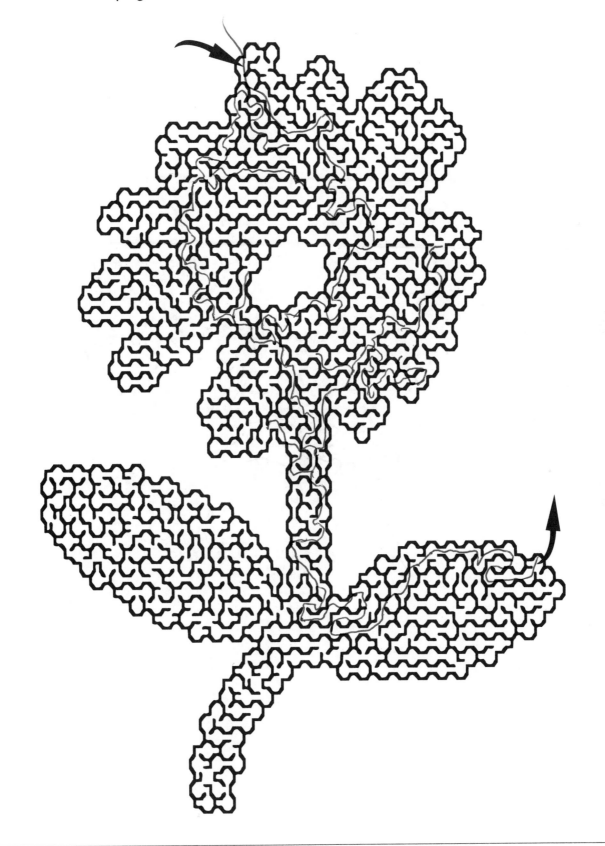

Flower 7

Solution on page 266

Flower 8

Solution on page 266

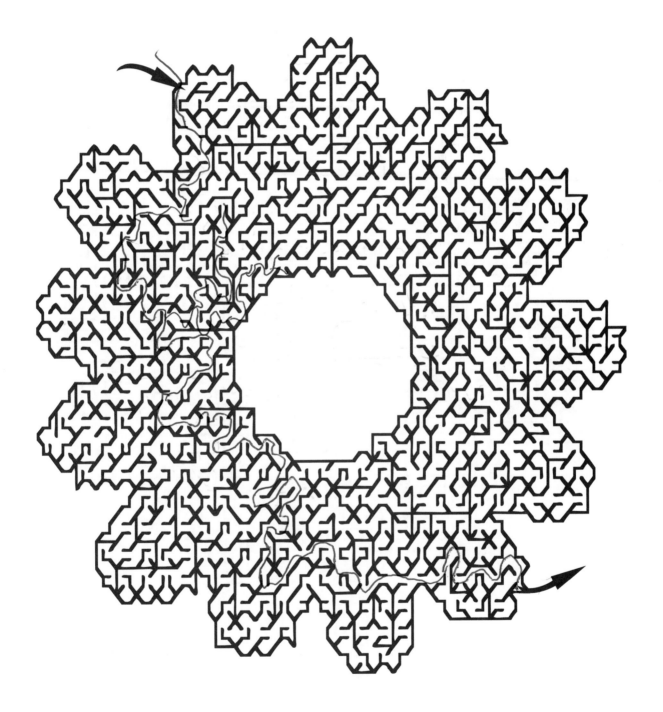

Flower 9

Solution on page 267

Flower 10

Solution on page 267

Bubbles 1

Solution on page 267

Bubbles 2

Solution on page 267

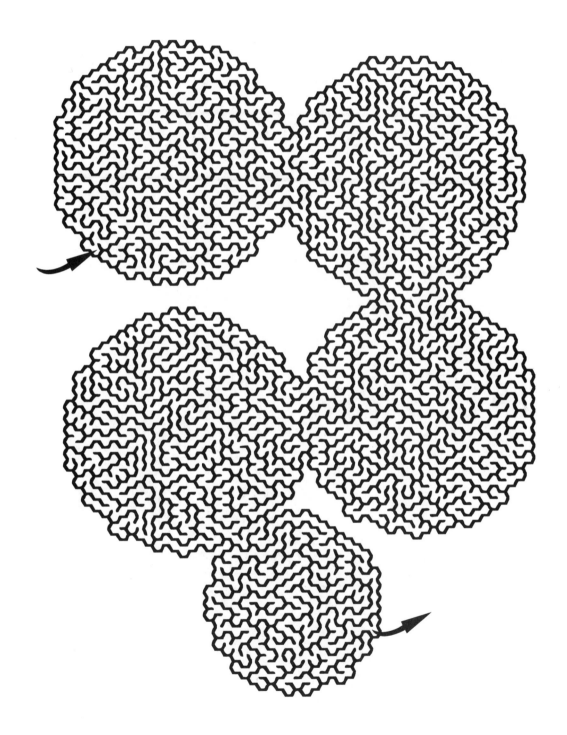

Bubbles 3

Solution on page 268

Bubbles 4

Solution on page 268

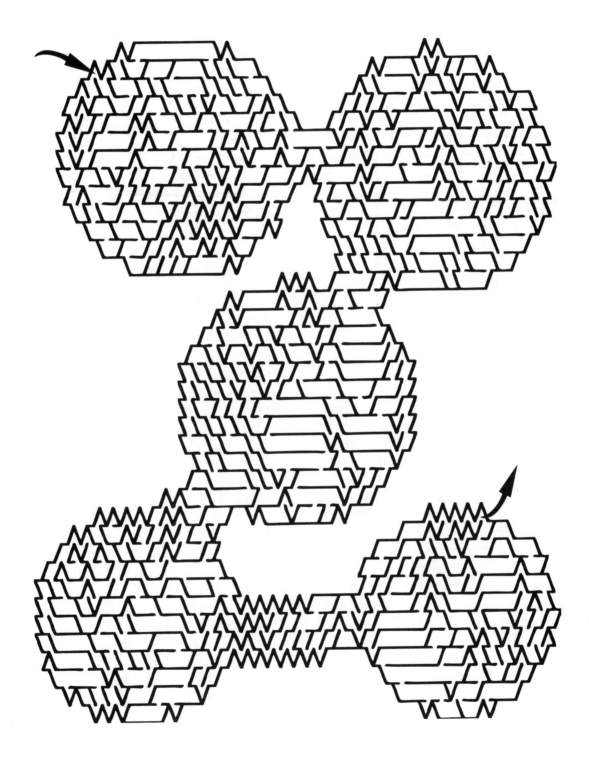

Bubbles 5

Solution on page 268

Bubbles 6

Solution on page 268

Bubbles 7

Solution on page 269

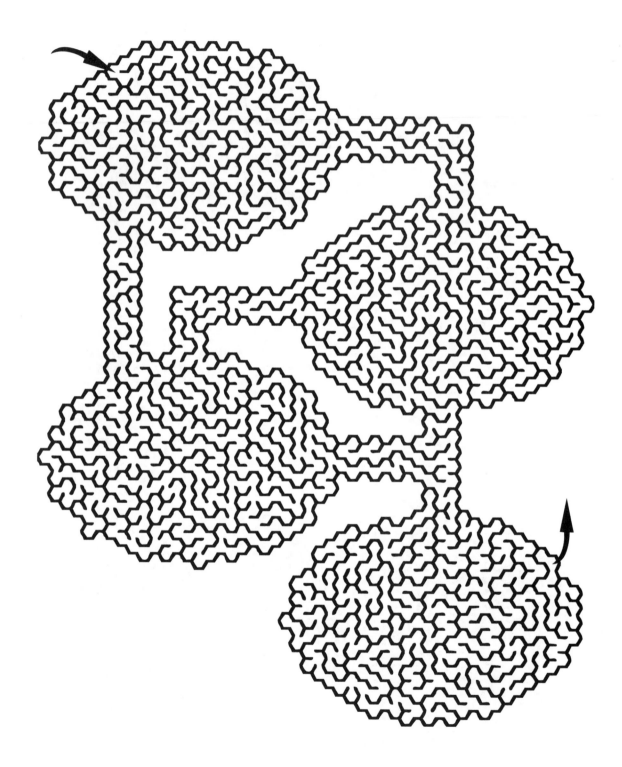

Bubbles 8

Solution on page 269

Bubbles 9

Solution on page 269

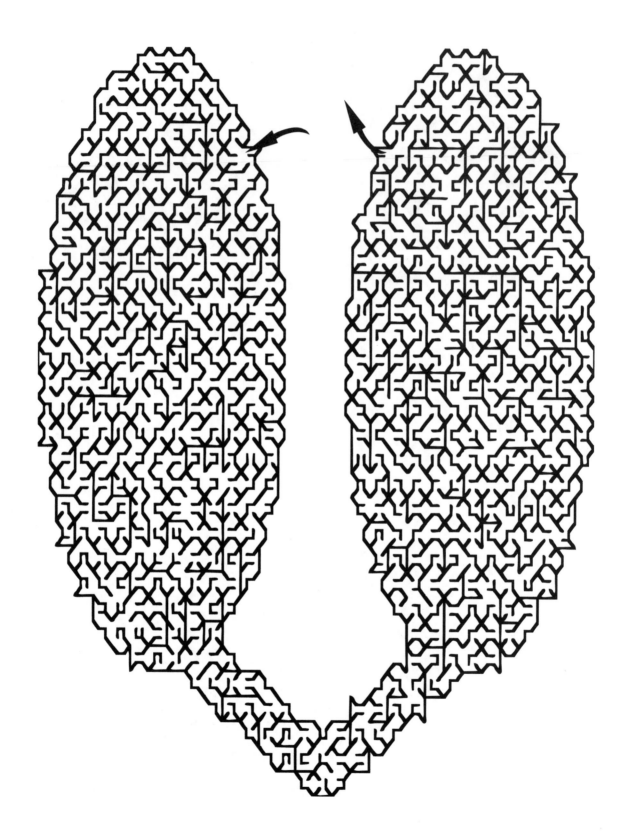

Bubbles 10

Solution on page 269

Bubbles 11

Solution on page 270

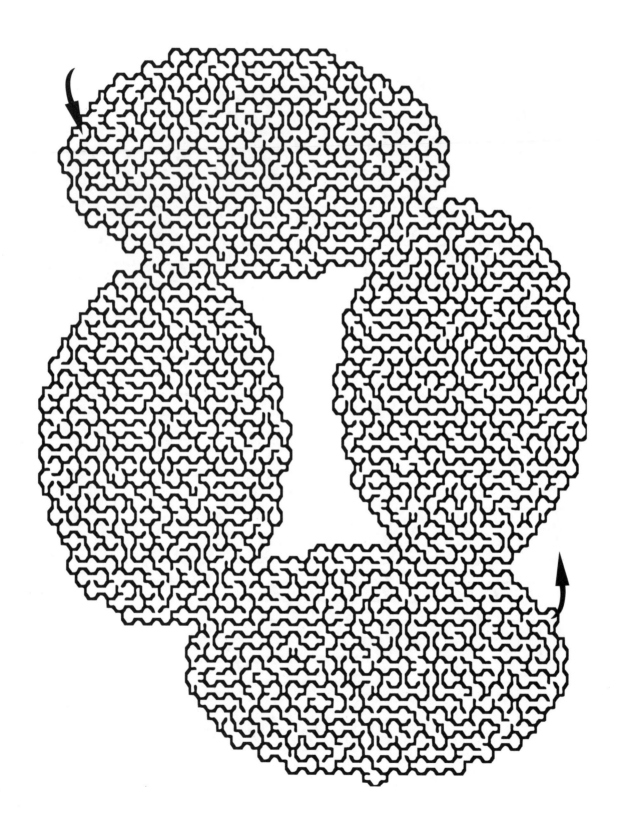

Blueprint 1

Solution on page 270

Blueprint 2

Solution on page 270

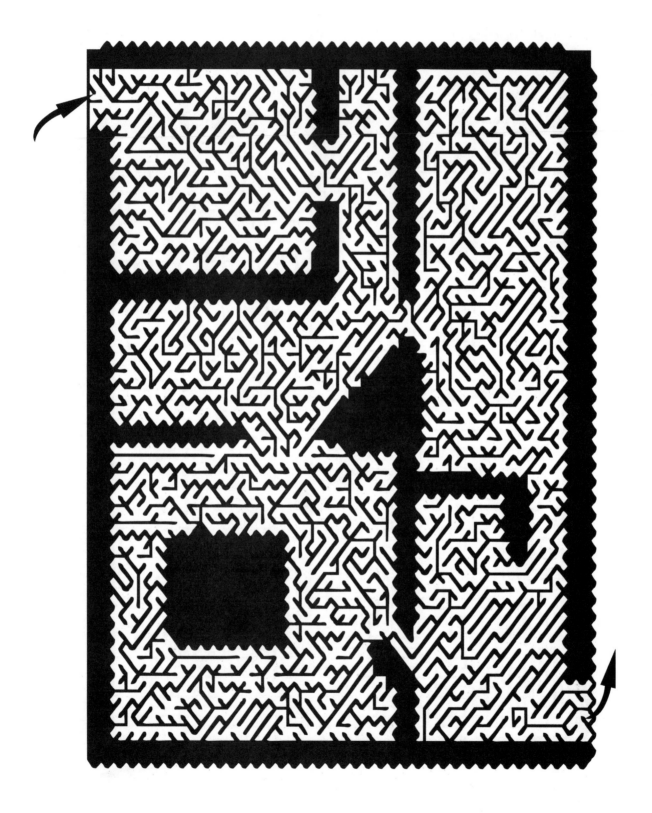

Blueprint 3

Solution on page 271

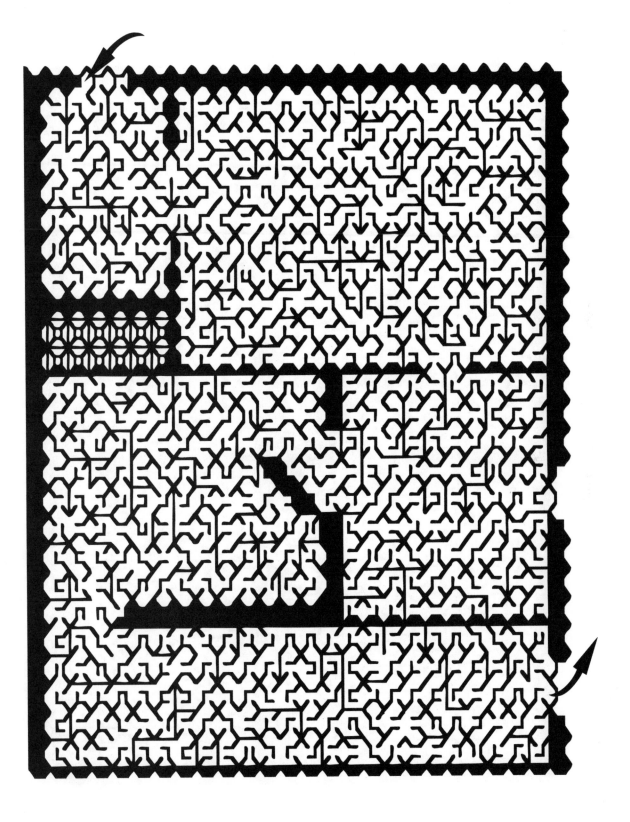

Blueprint 4

Solution on page 271

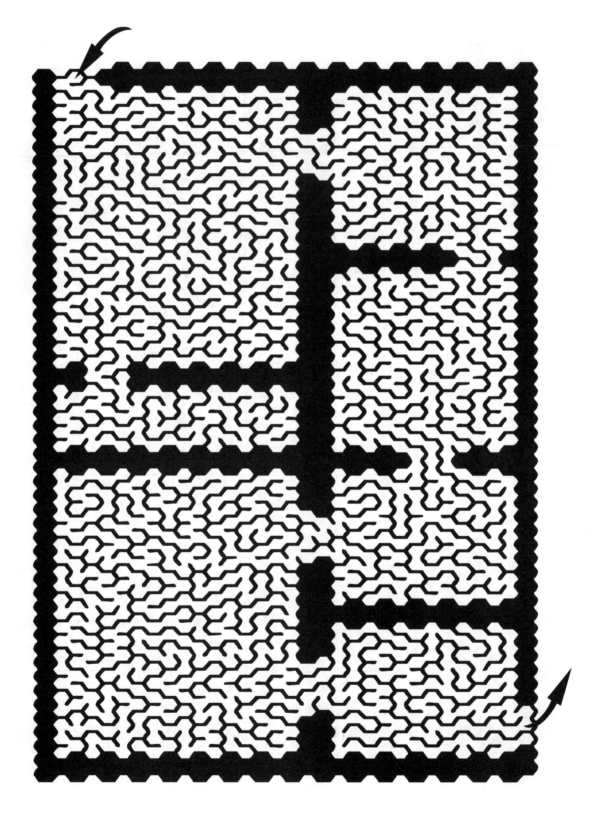

Blueprint 5

Solution on page 271

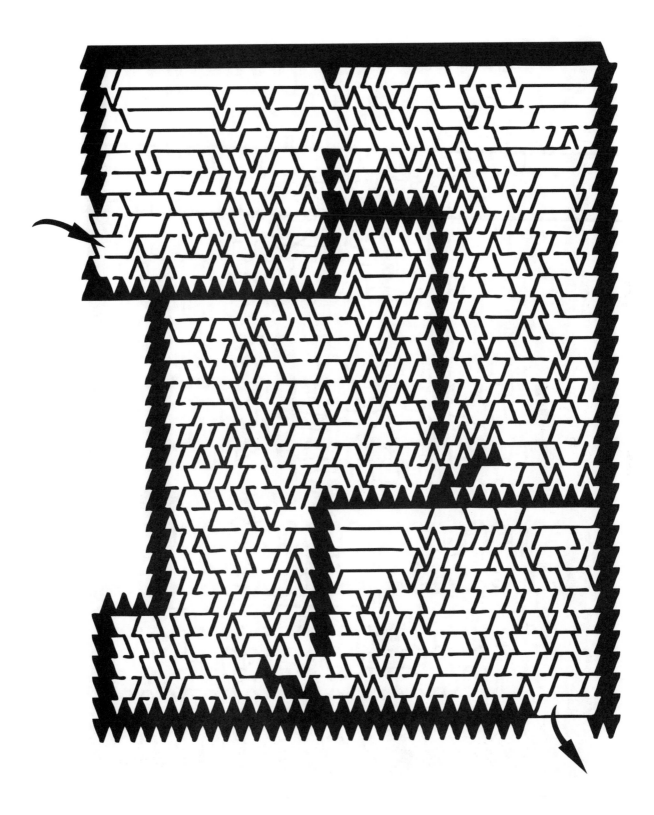

Blueprint 6

Solution on page 271

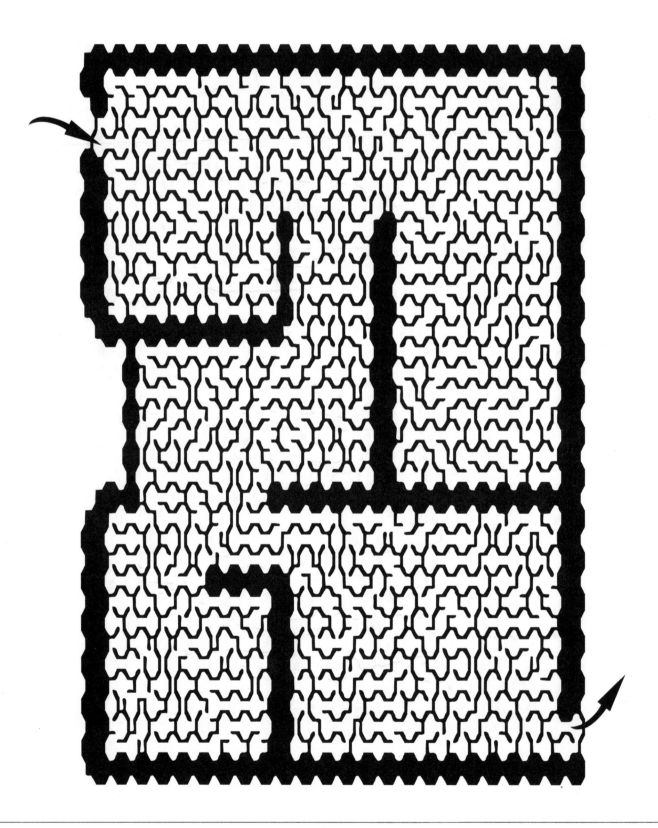

Blueprint 7

Solution on page 272

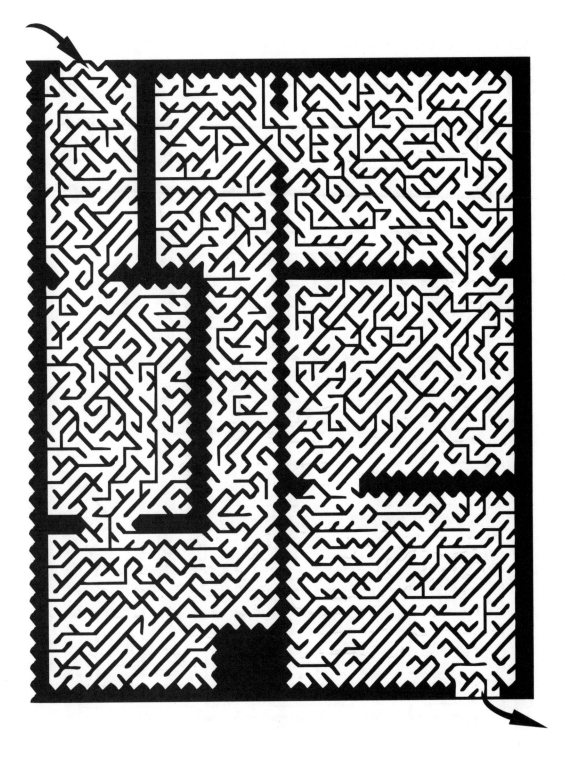

Blueprint 8

Solution on page 272

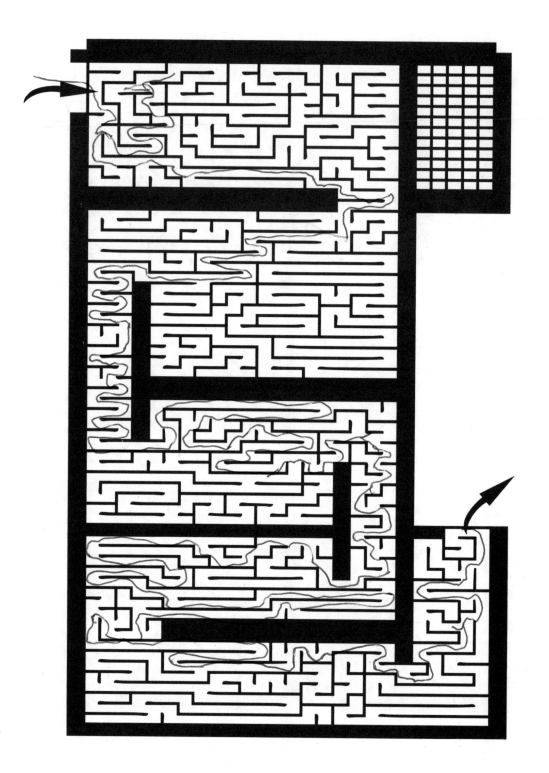

Blueprint 9

Solution on page 272

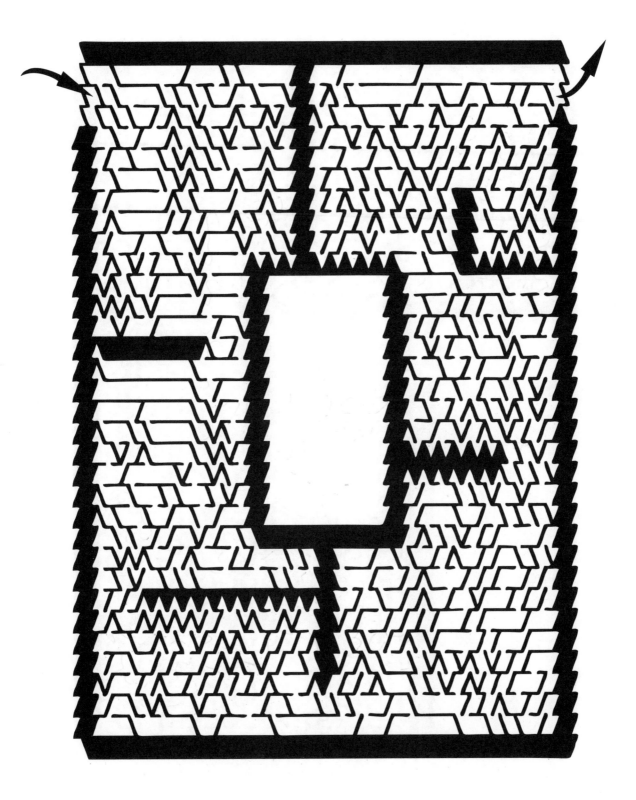

Blueprint 10

Solution on page 272

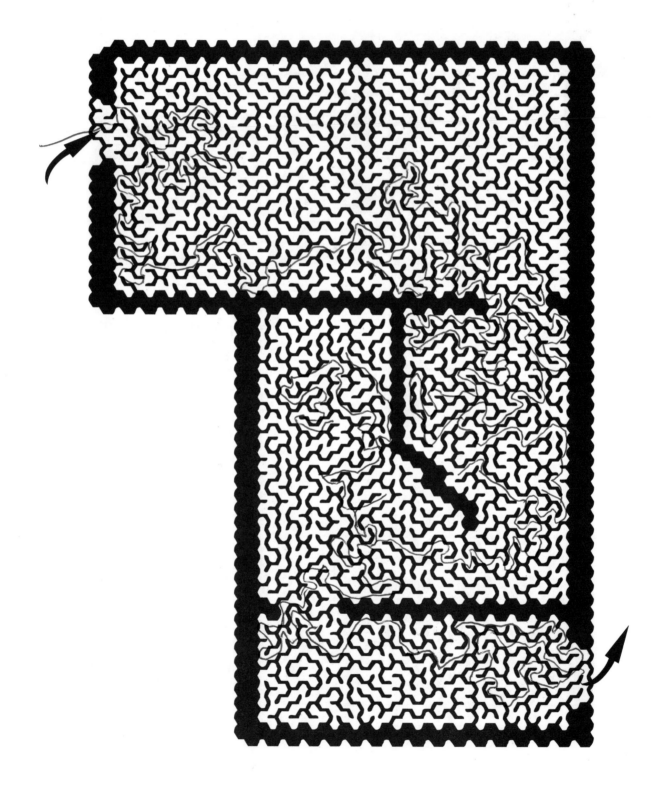

Blueprint 11

Solution on page 273

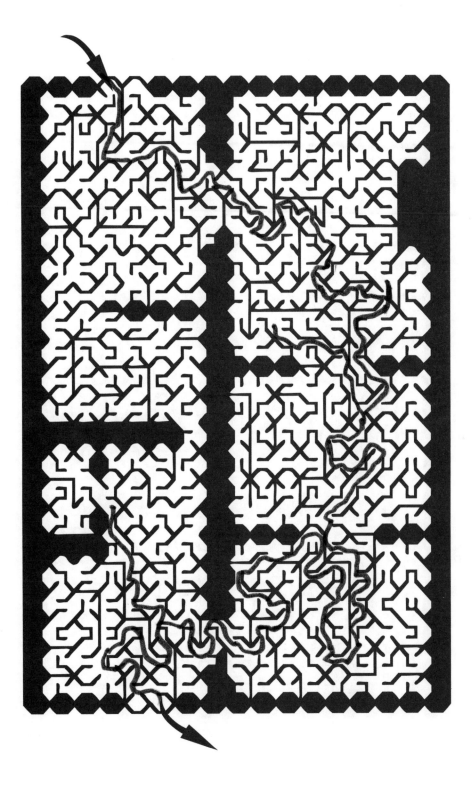

Blueprint 12

Solution on page 273

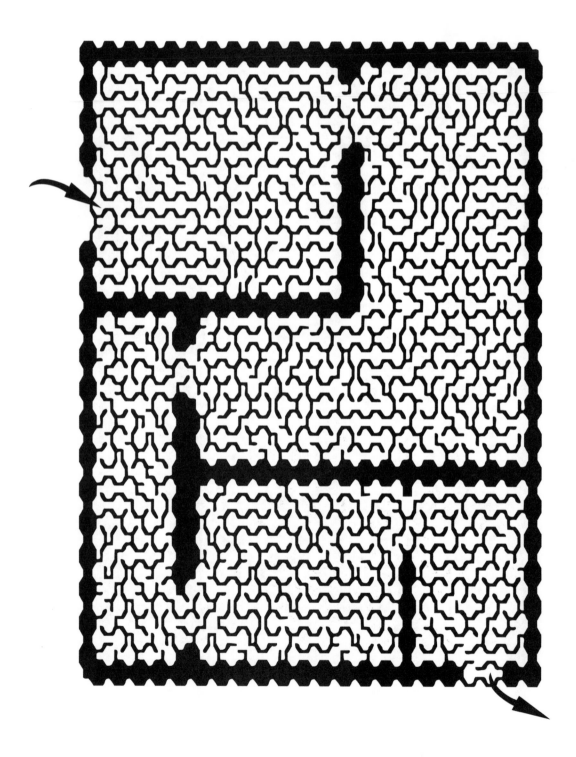

Chapter 17: Cups Full of Mazes

Cup 1

Solution on page 273

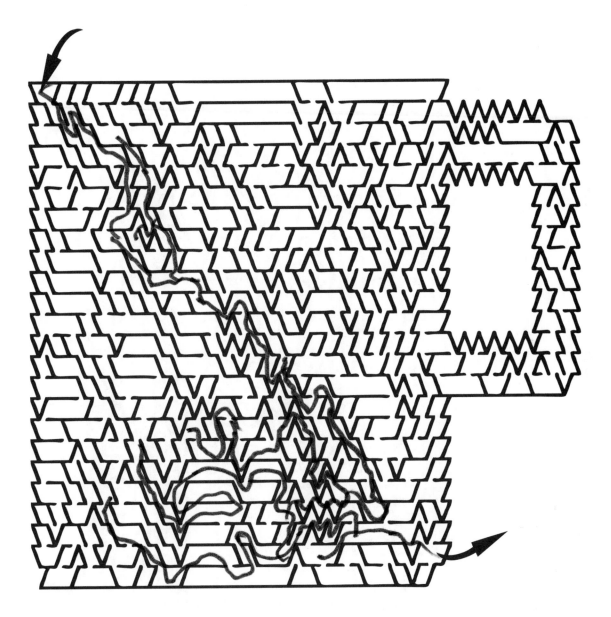

Cup 2

Solution on page 273

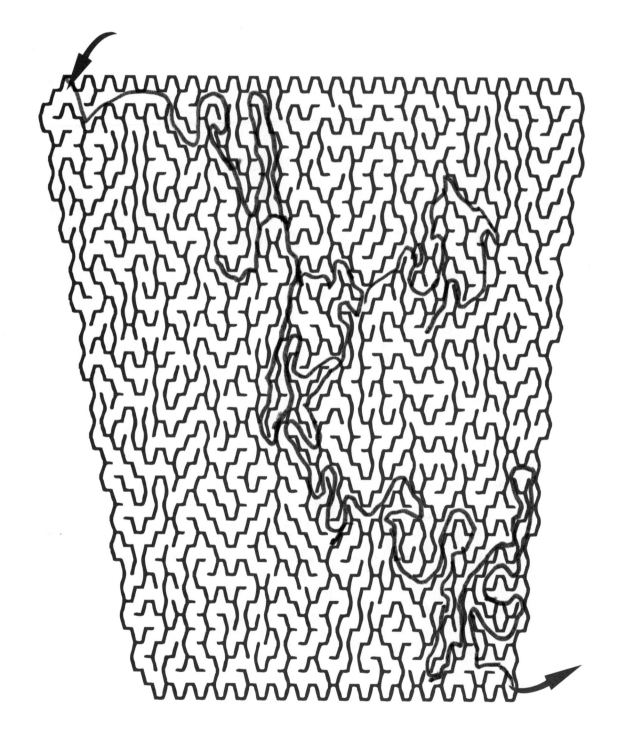

Cup 3

Solution on page 274

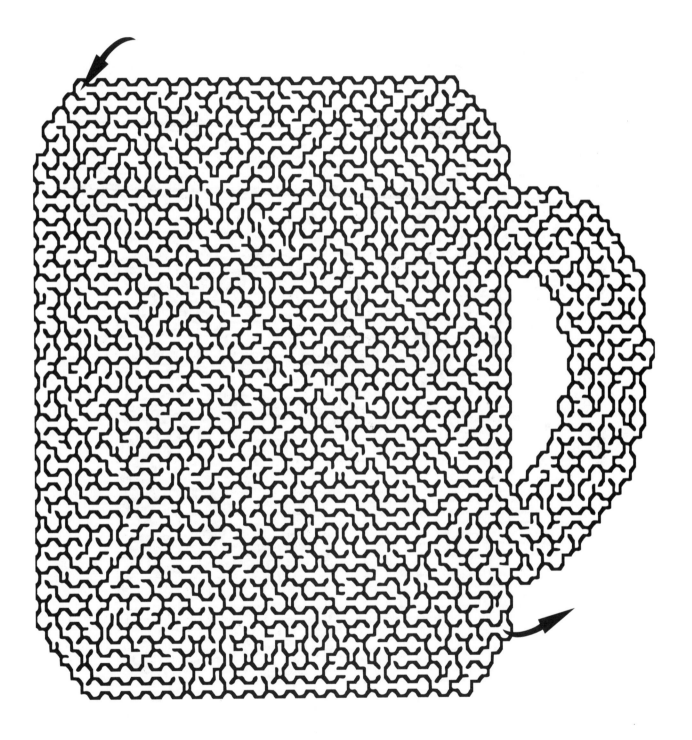

Cup 4

Solution on page 274

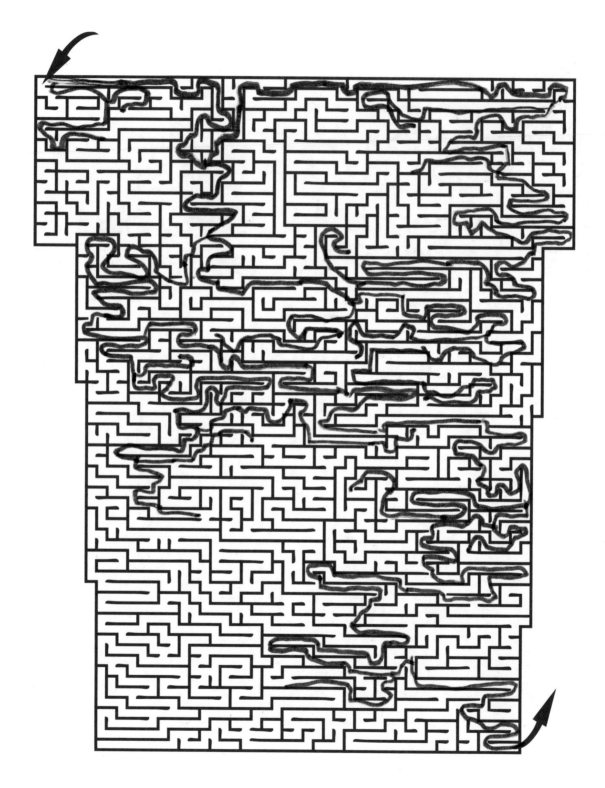

Cup 5

Solution on page 274

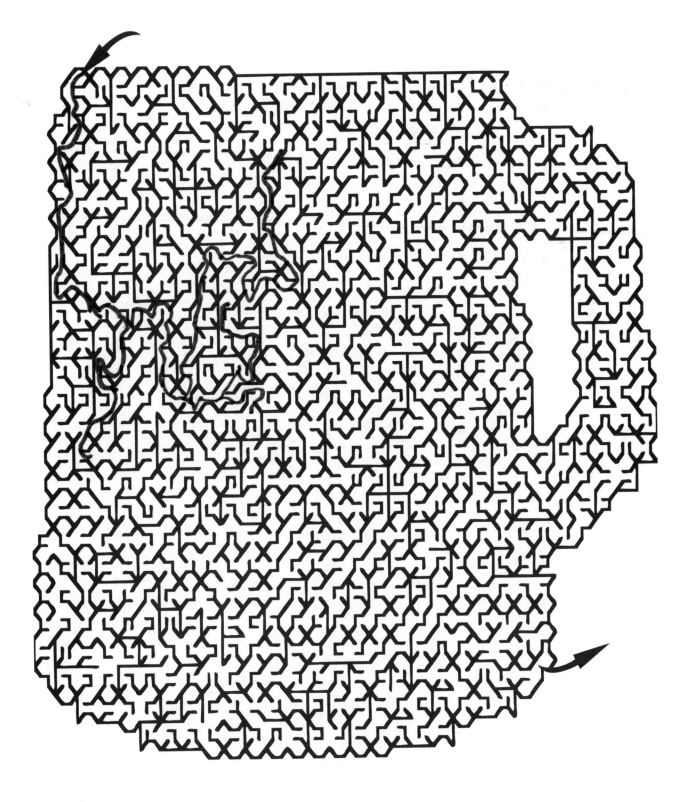

Cup 6

Solution on page 274

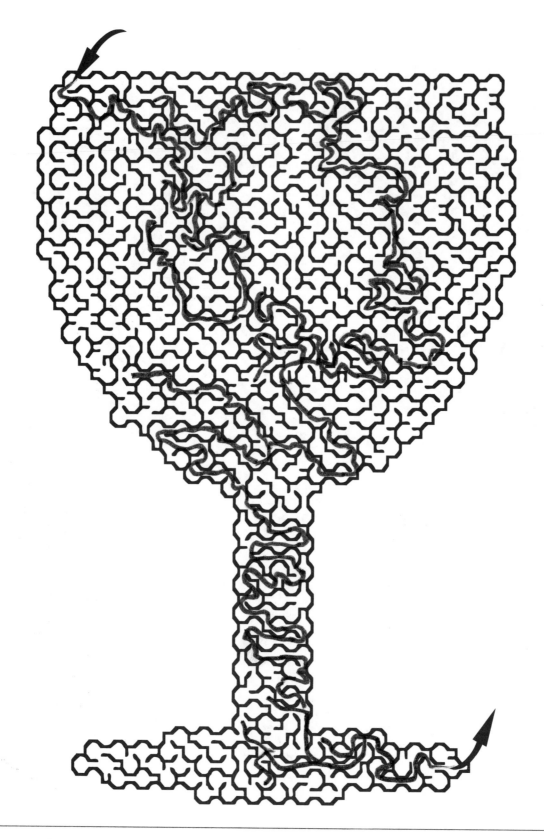

Cup 7

Solution on page 275

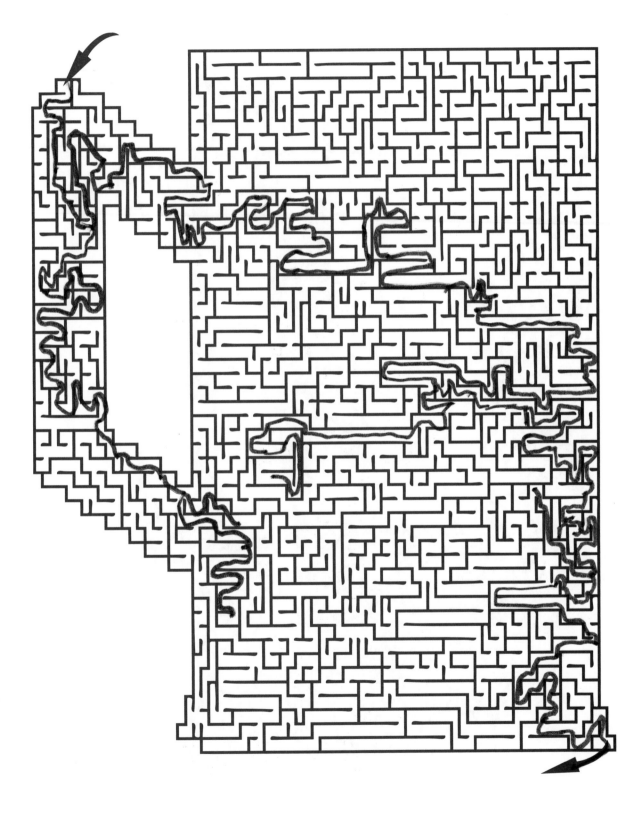

Cup 8

Solution on page 275

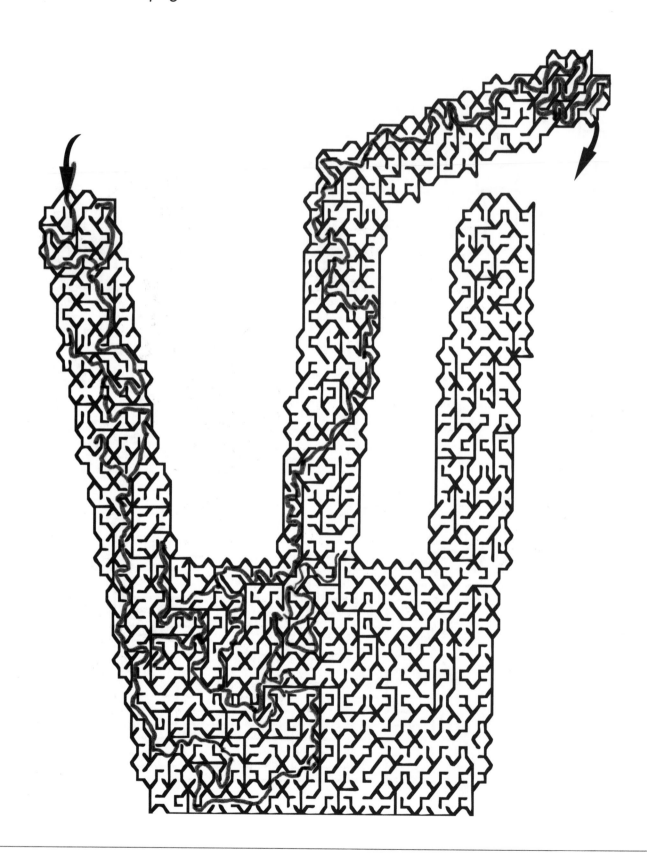

Cup 9

Solution on page 275

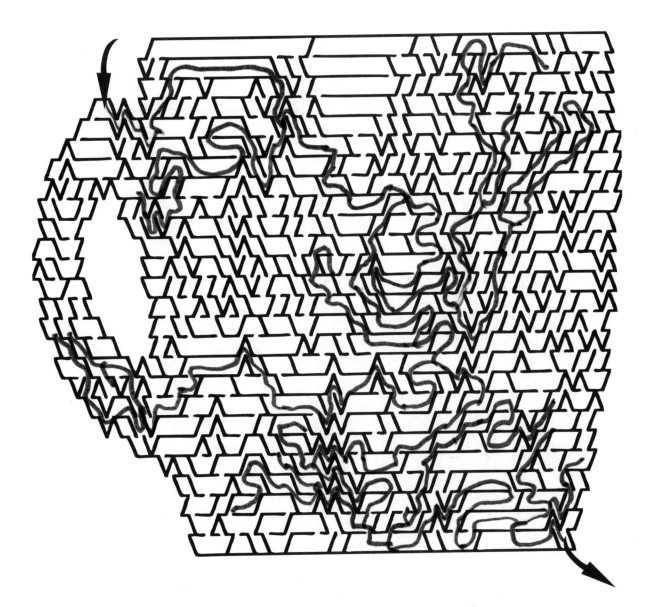

Arrowhead 1

Solution on page 276

Arrowhead 2

Solution on page 276

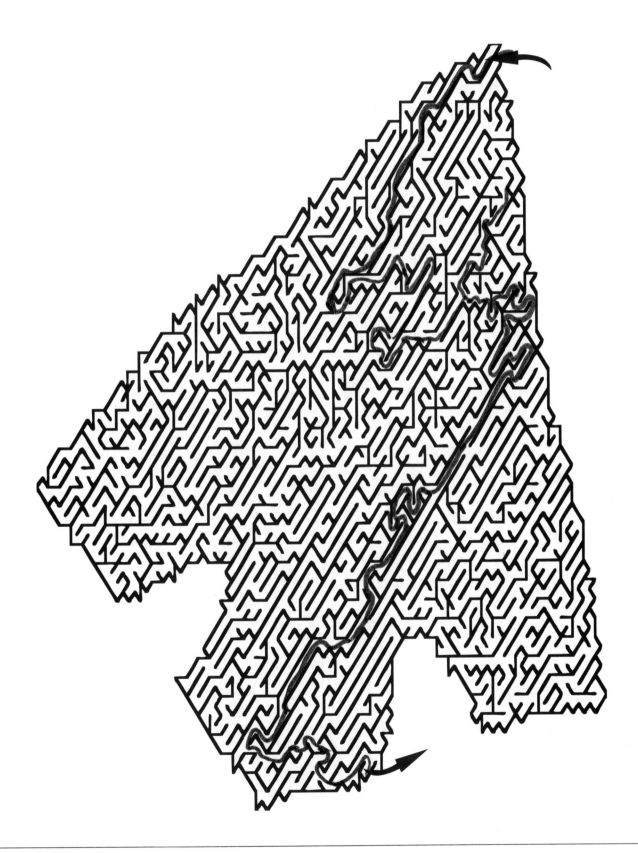

Arrowhead 3

Solution on page 276

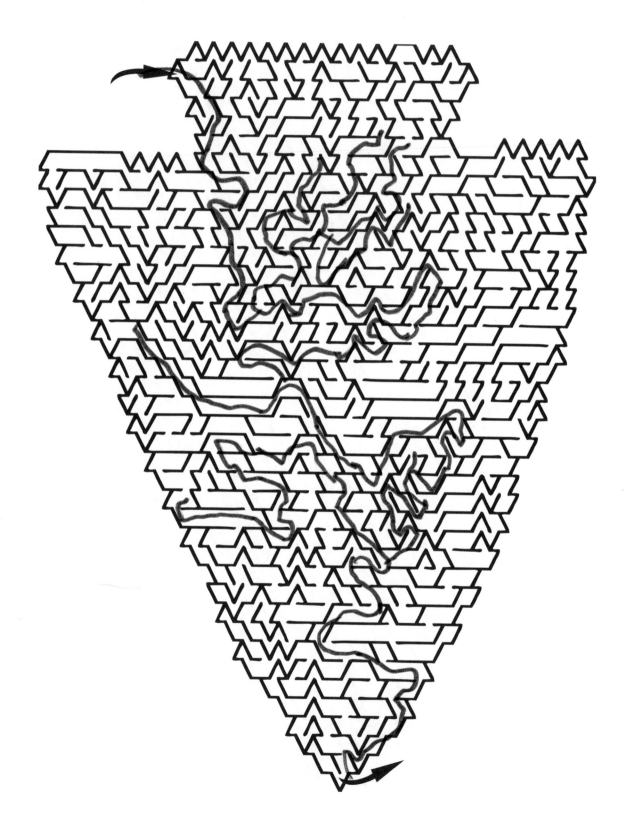

Arrowhead 4

Solution on page 276

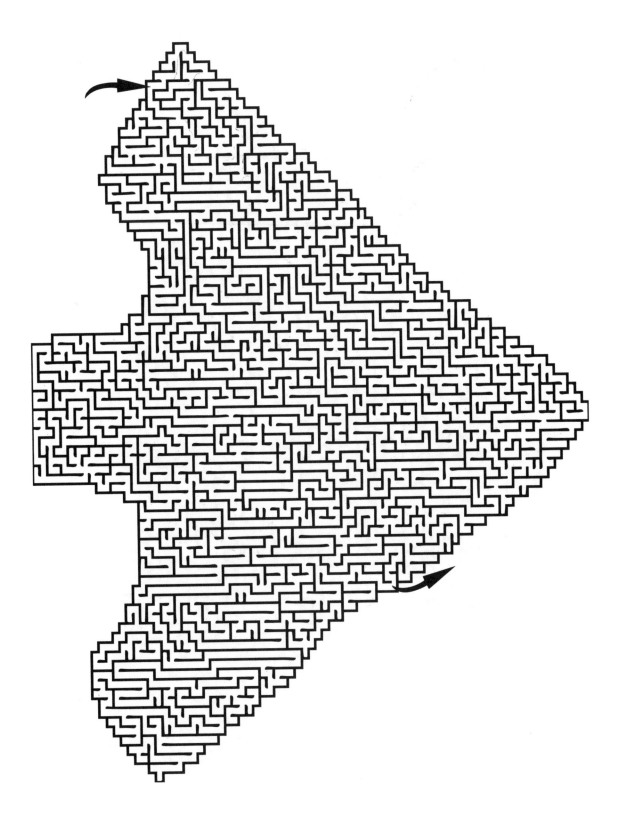

Arrowhead 5

Solution on page 277

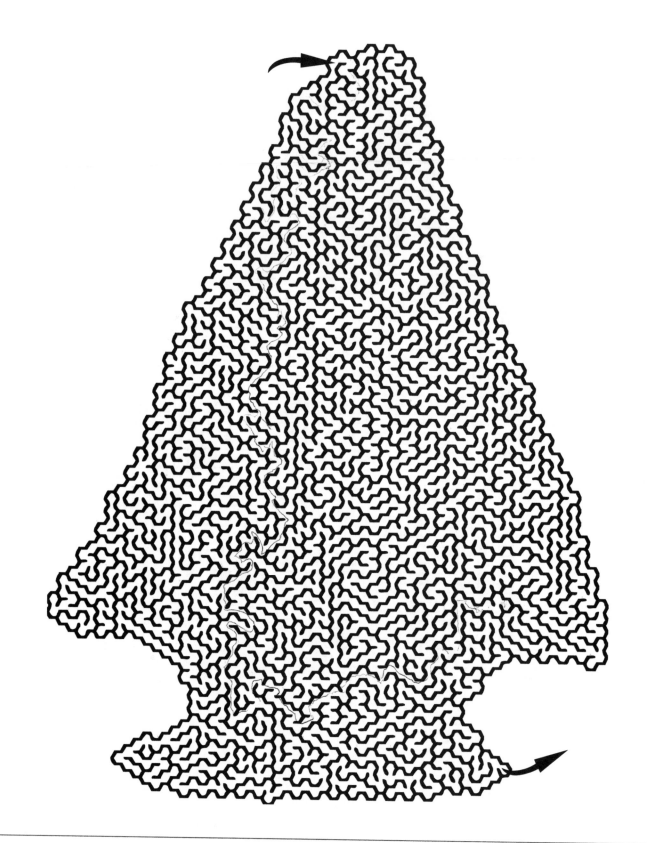

Arrowhead 6

Solution on page 277

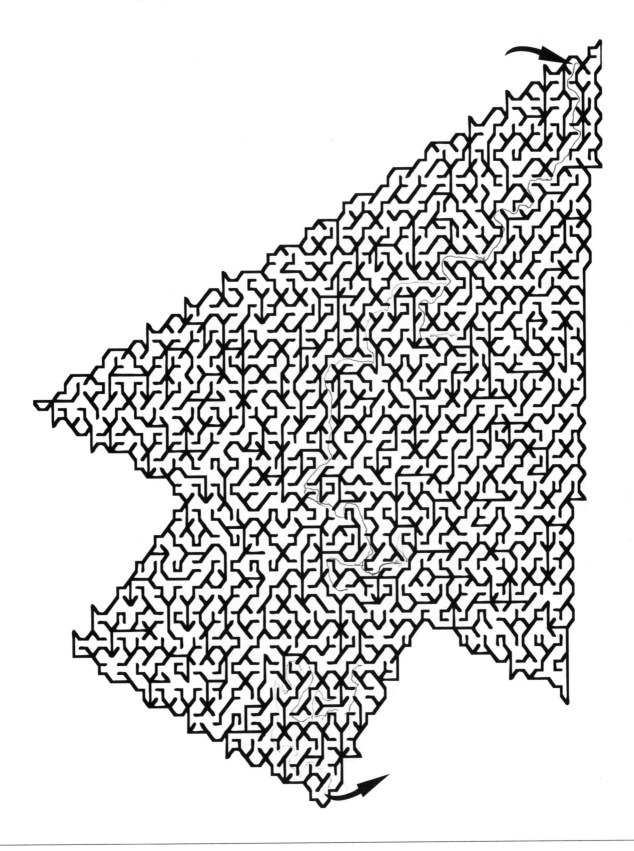

Arrowhead 7

Solution on page 277

Arrowhead 8

Solution on page 277

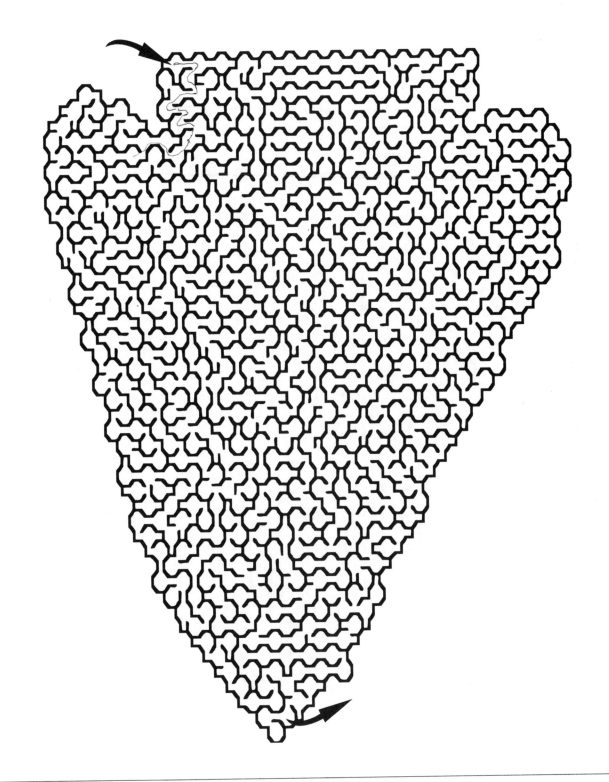

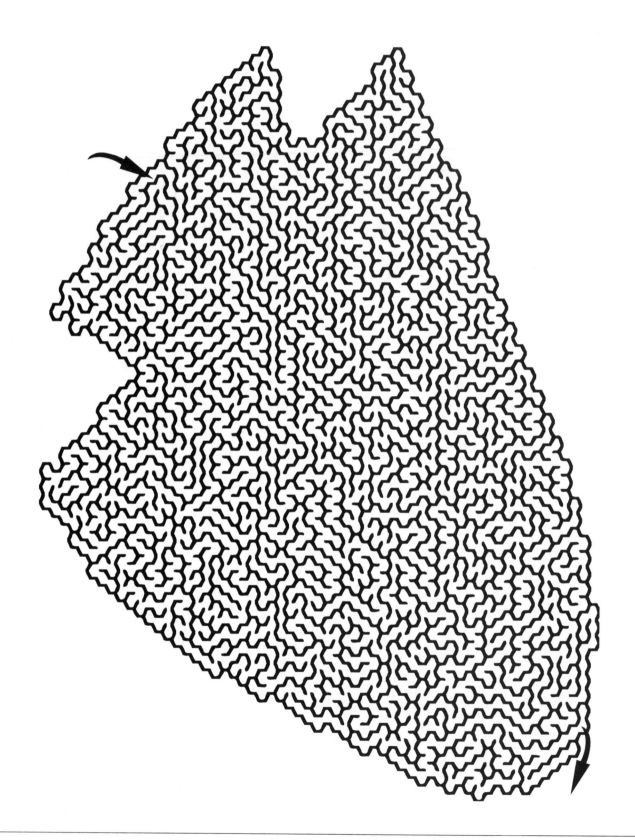

Arrowhead 10

Solution on page 278

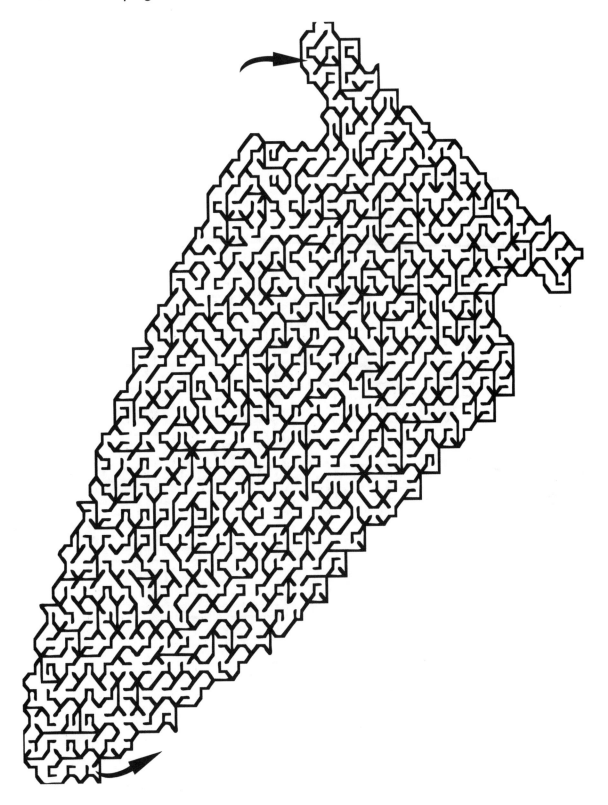

Mitten

Solution on page 278

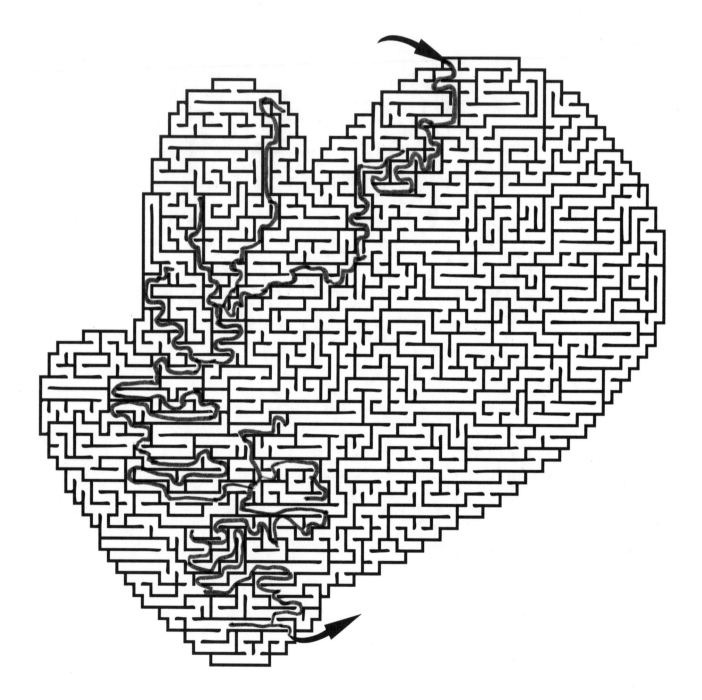

Shorts

Solution on page 278

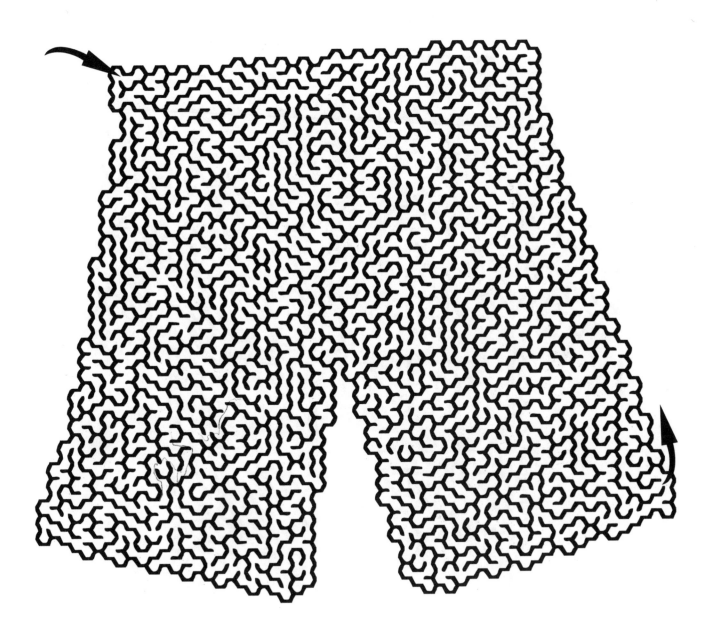

Jersey

Solution on page 279

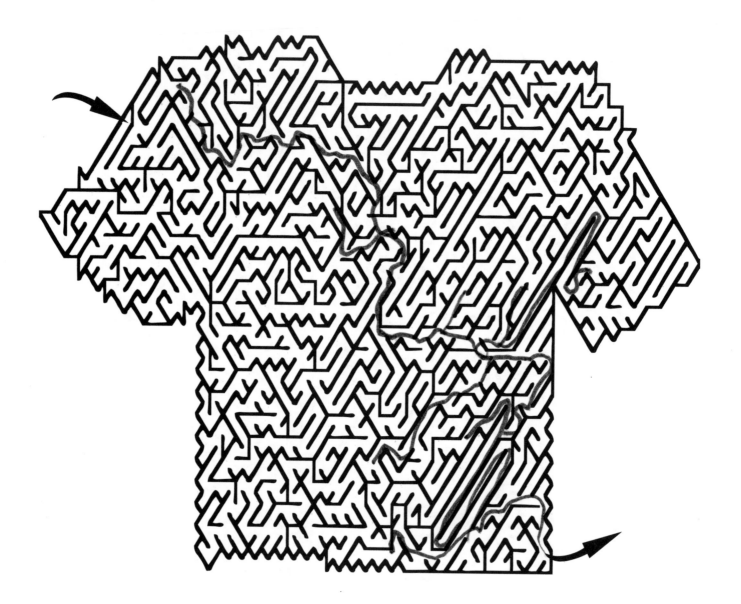

Boot

Solution on page 279

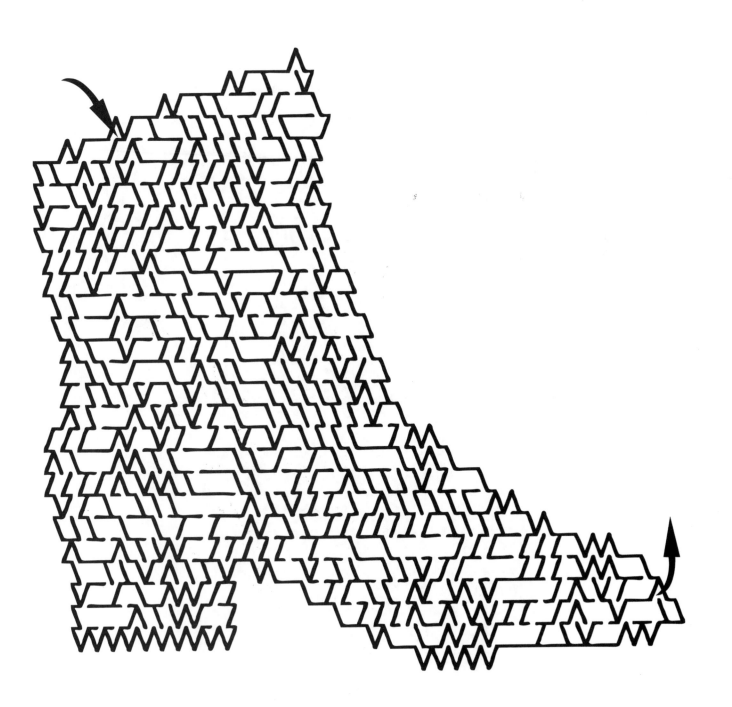

Dress

Solution on page 279

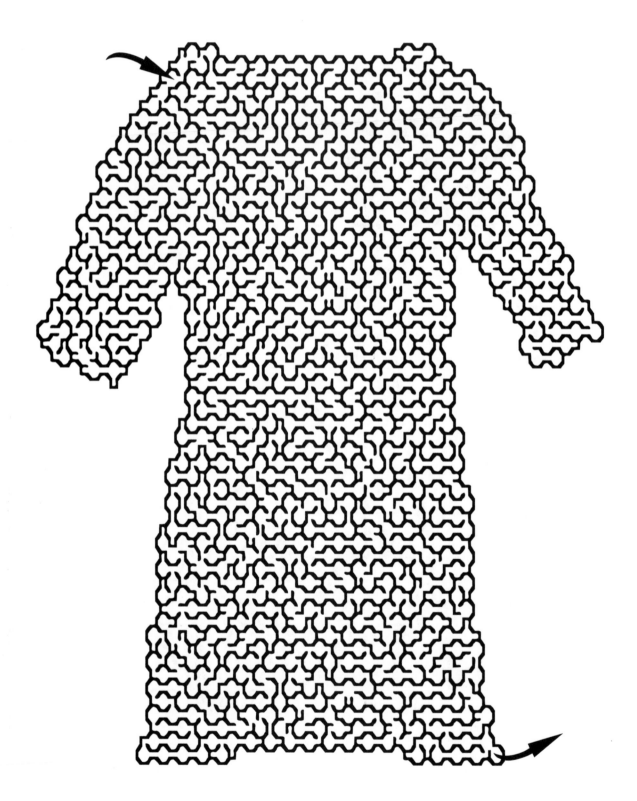

Tank Top

Solution on page 279

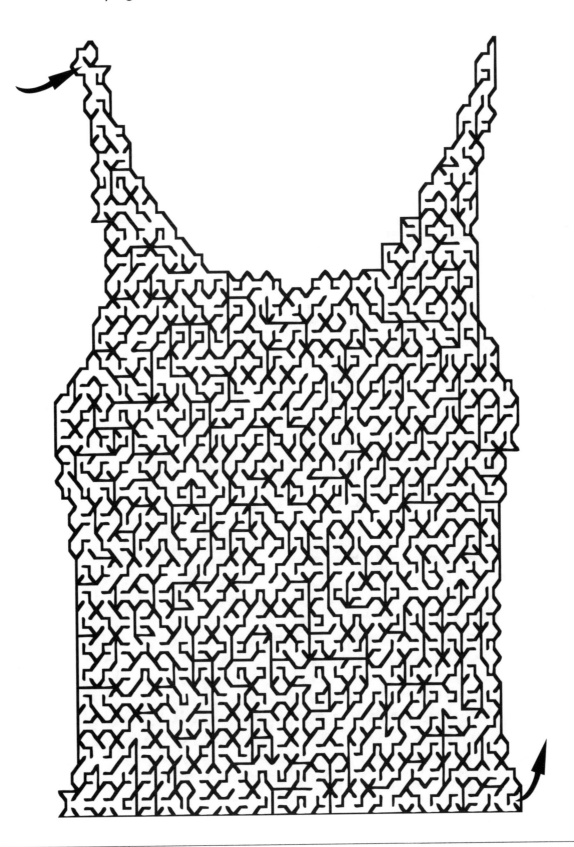

Party Hat

Solution on page 280

Pants

Solution on page 280

Glove

Solution on page 280

Shoe

Solution on page 280

Shirt

Solution on page 281

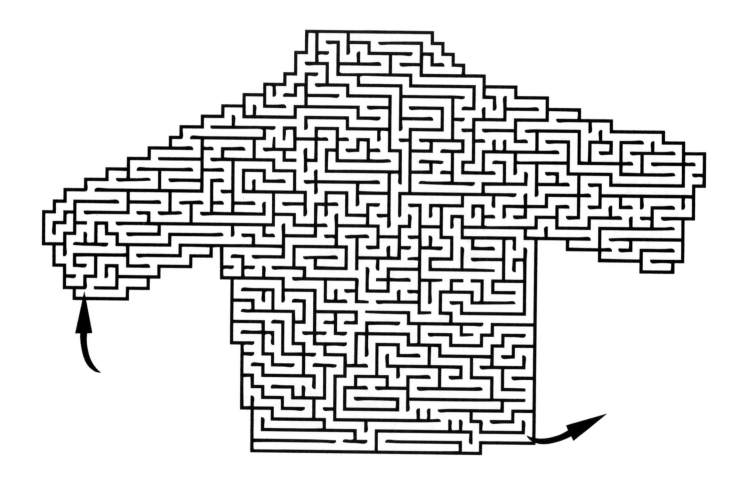

Fish 1

Solution on page 281

Fish 2

Solution on page 281

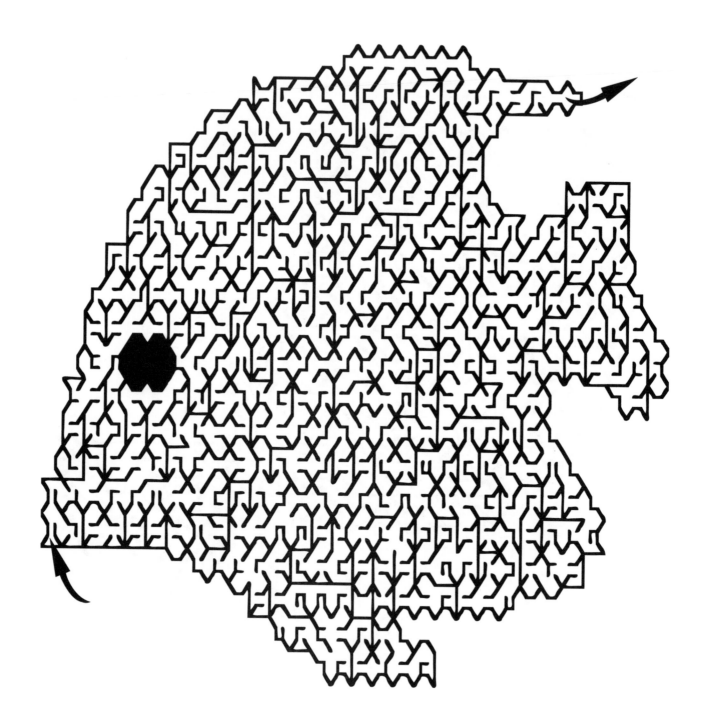

Fish 3

Solution on page 281

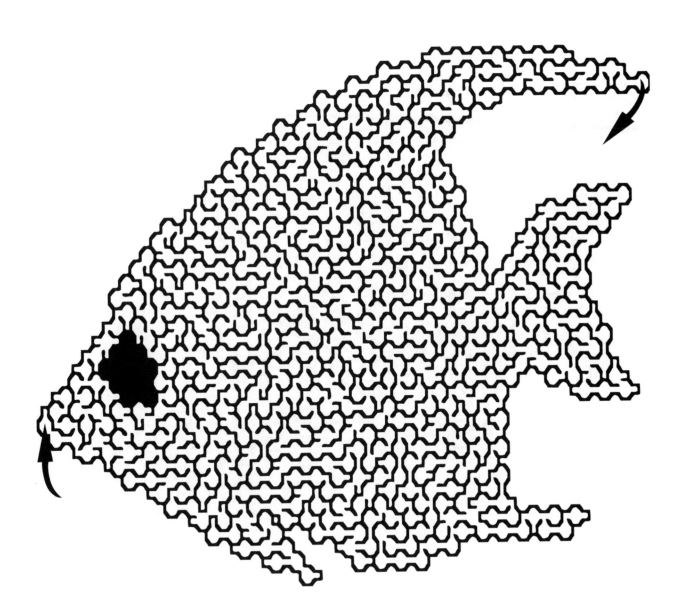

Fish 4

Solution on page 282

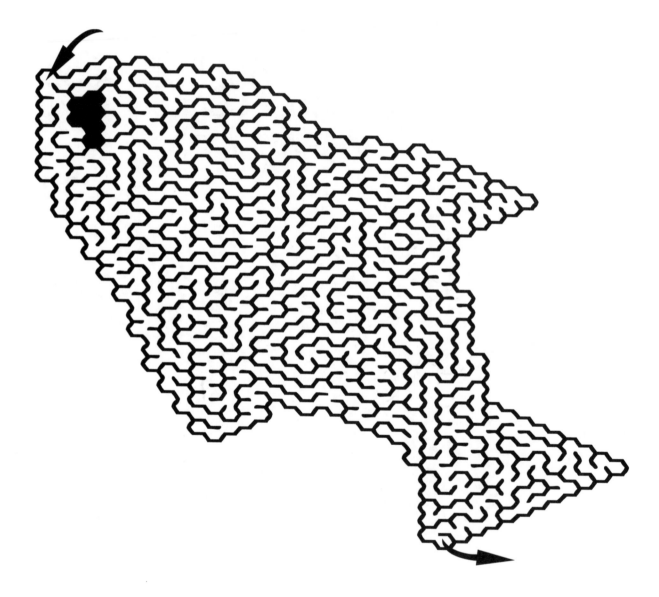

Fish 5

Solution on page 282

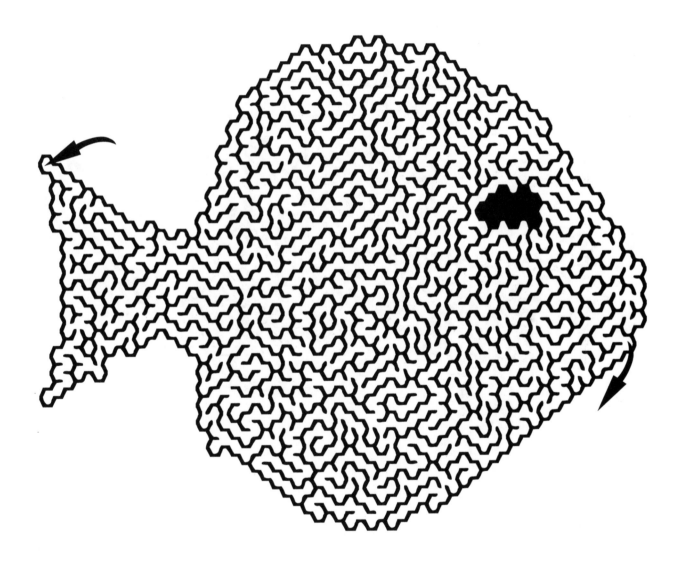

Fish 6

Solution on page 282

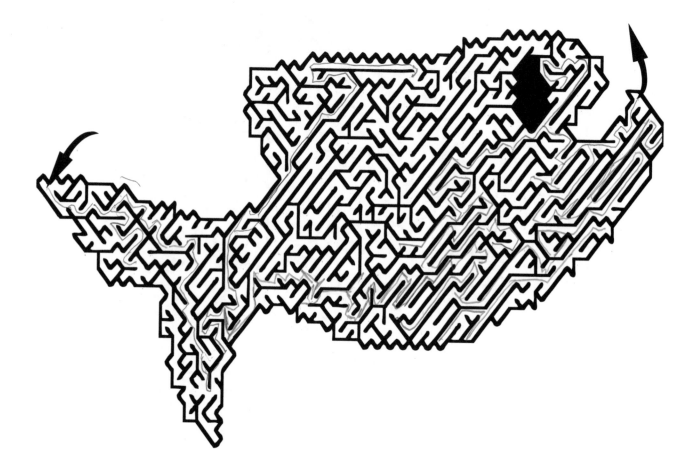

Fish 7

Solution on page 282

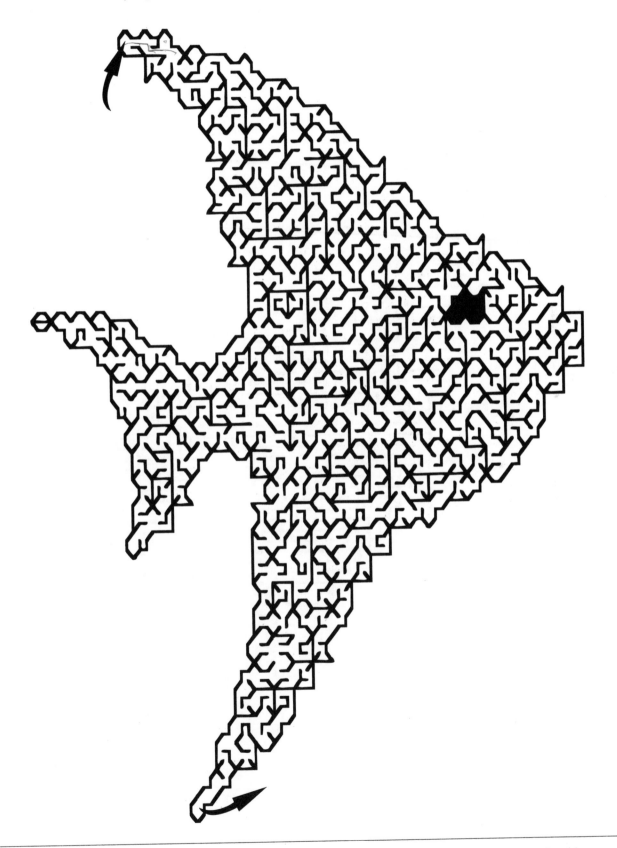

Fish 8

Solution on page 283

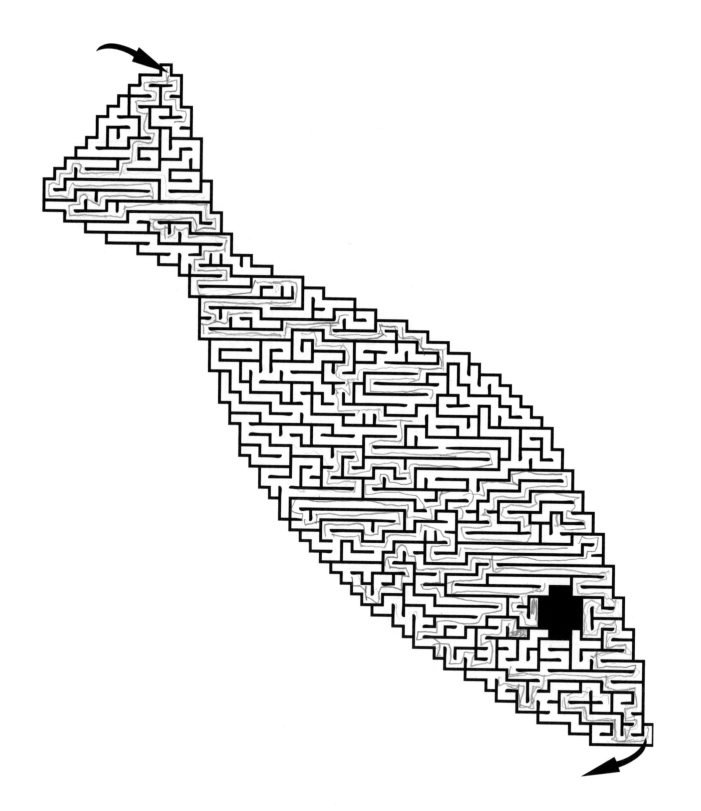

Fish 9

Solution on page 283

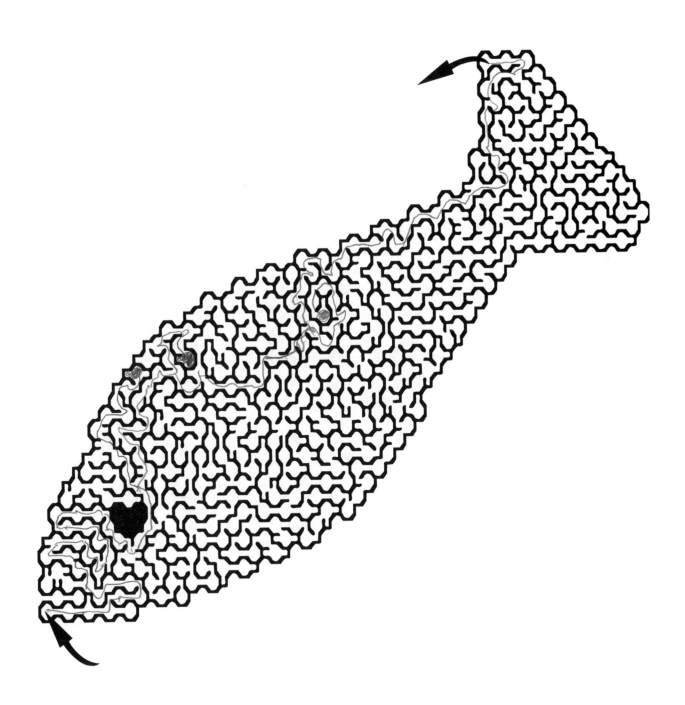

Fish 10

Solution on page 283

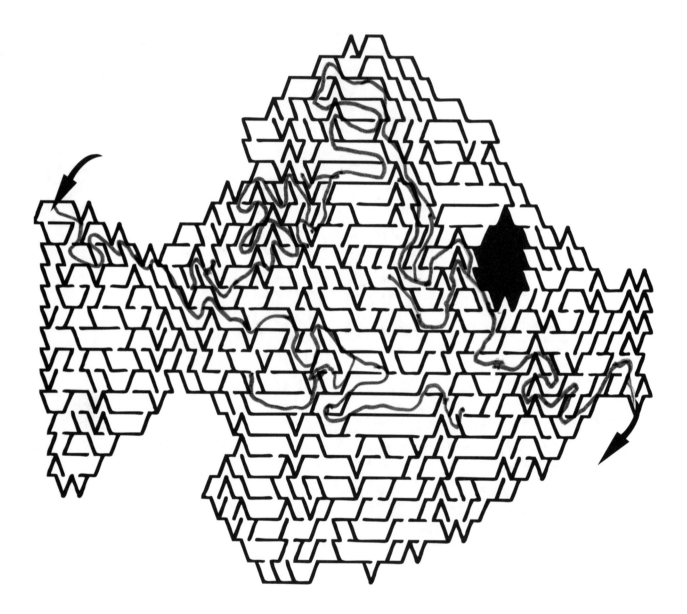

Pyramid 1

Solution on page 284

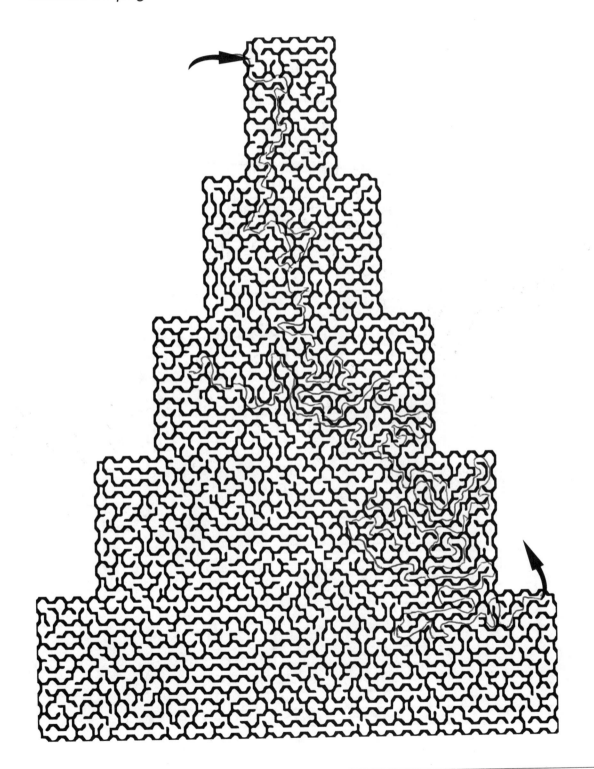

Pyramid 2

Solution on page 284

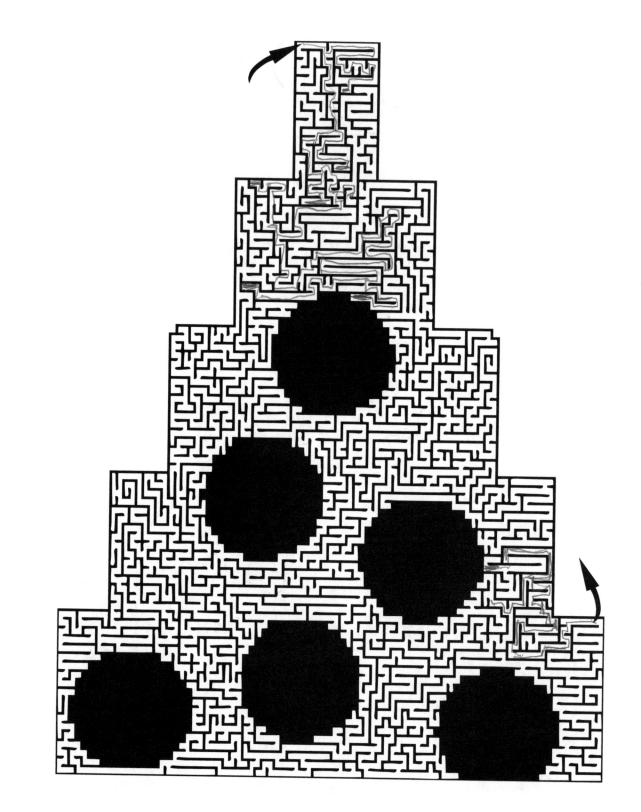

Pyramid 3

Solution on page 284

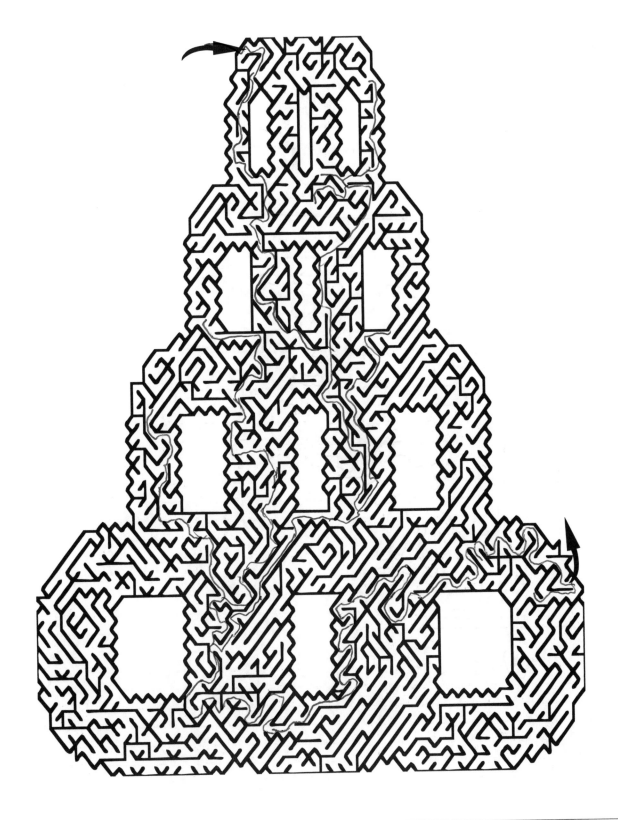

Pyramid 4

Solution on page 284

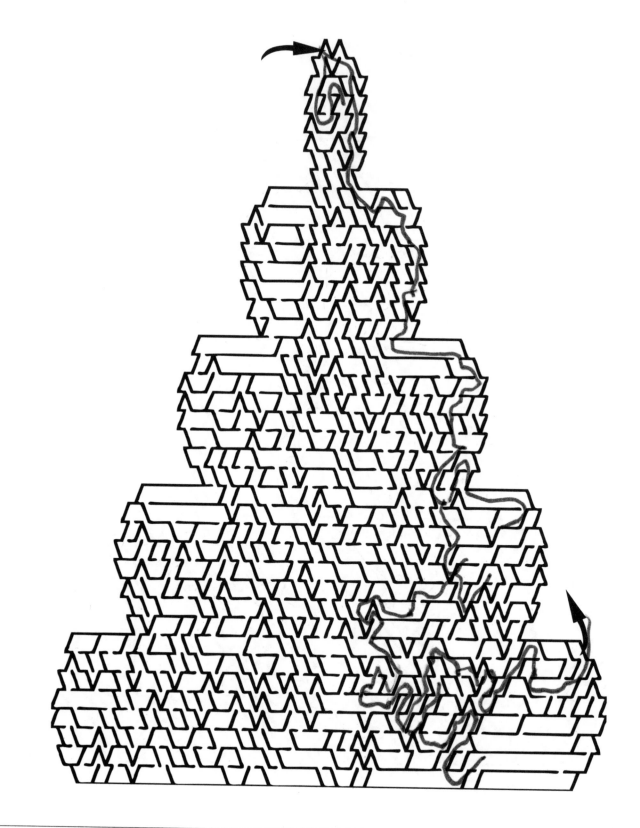

Pyramid 5

Solution on page 285

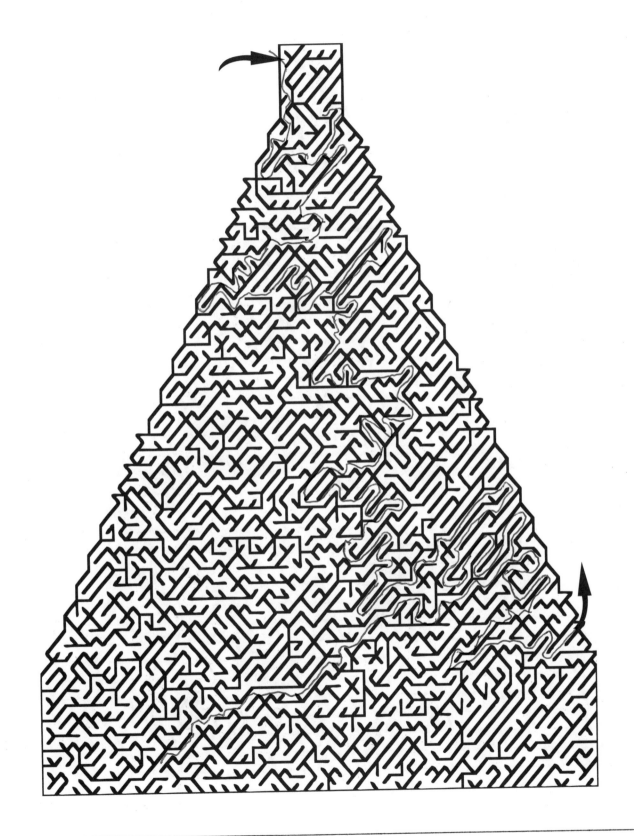

Pyramid 6

Solution on page 285

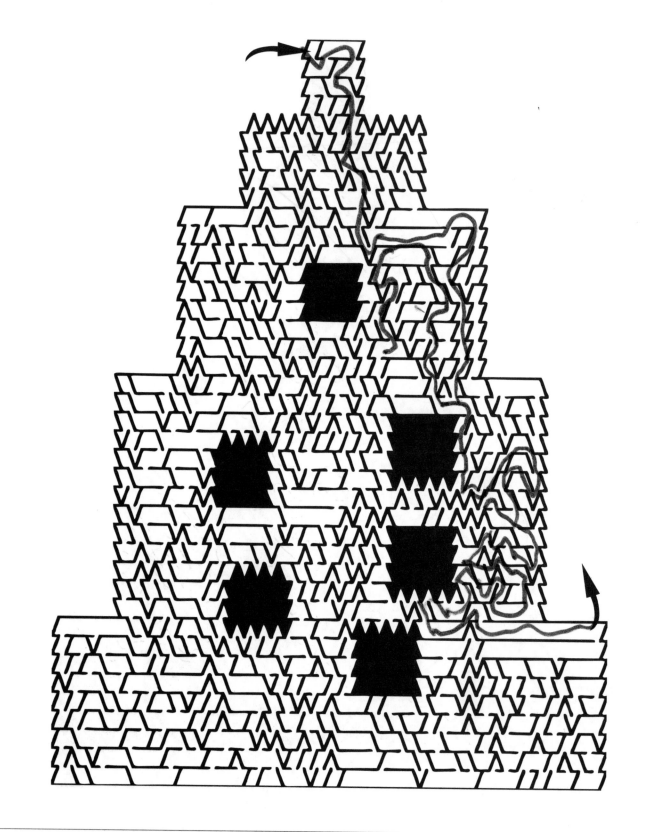

Pyramid 7

Solution on page 285

Pyramid 8

Solution on page 285

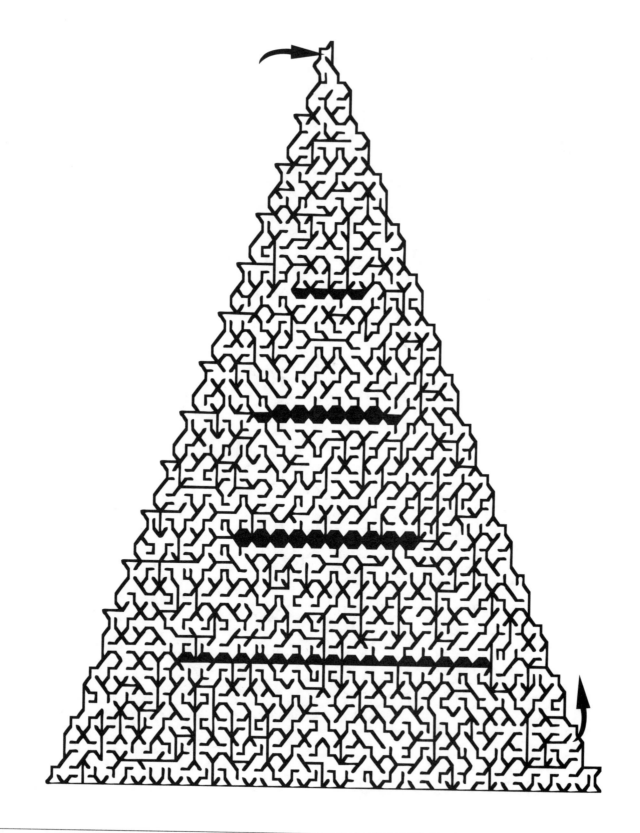

Leaf 1

Solution on page 286

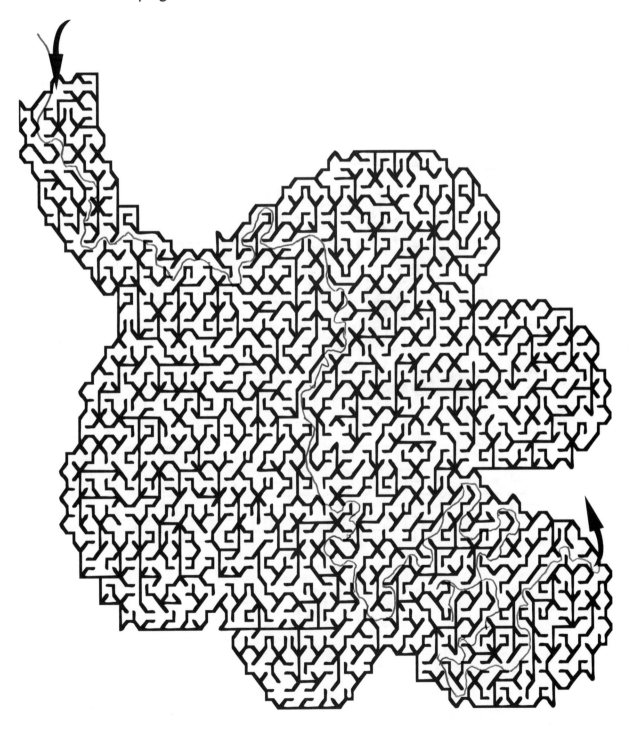

Leaf 2

Solution on page 286

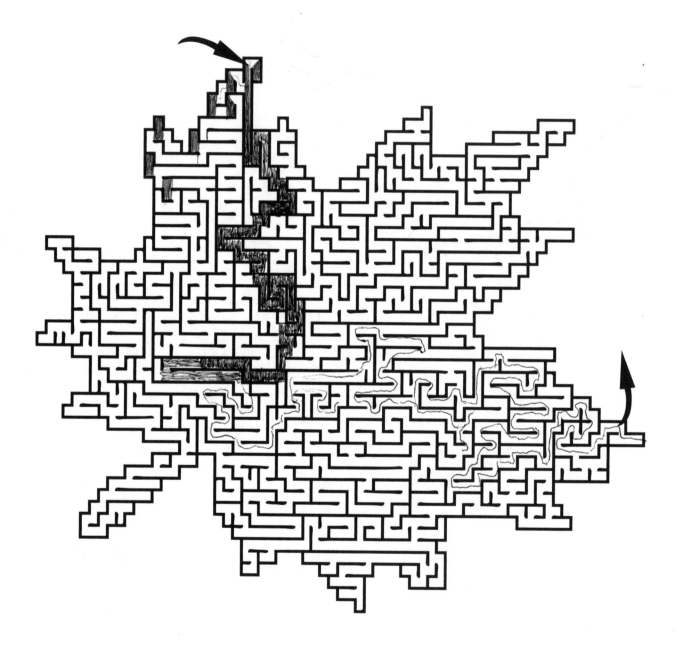

Leaf 3

Solution on page 286

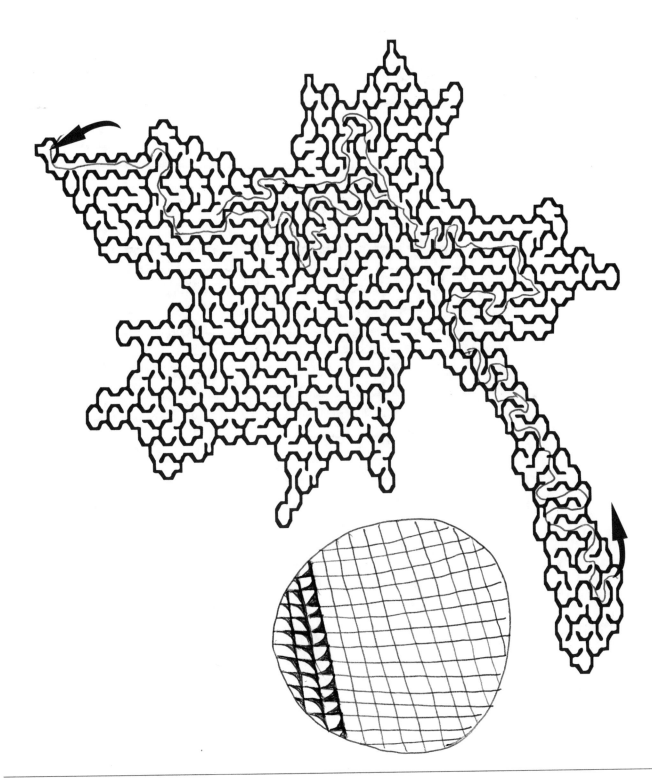

Leaf 4

Solution on page 286

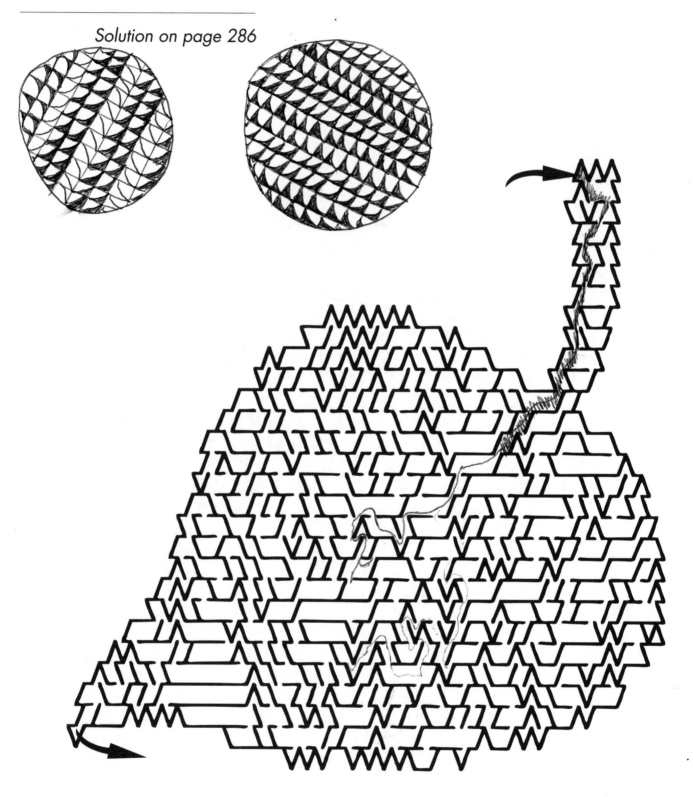

Leaf 5

Solution on page 287

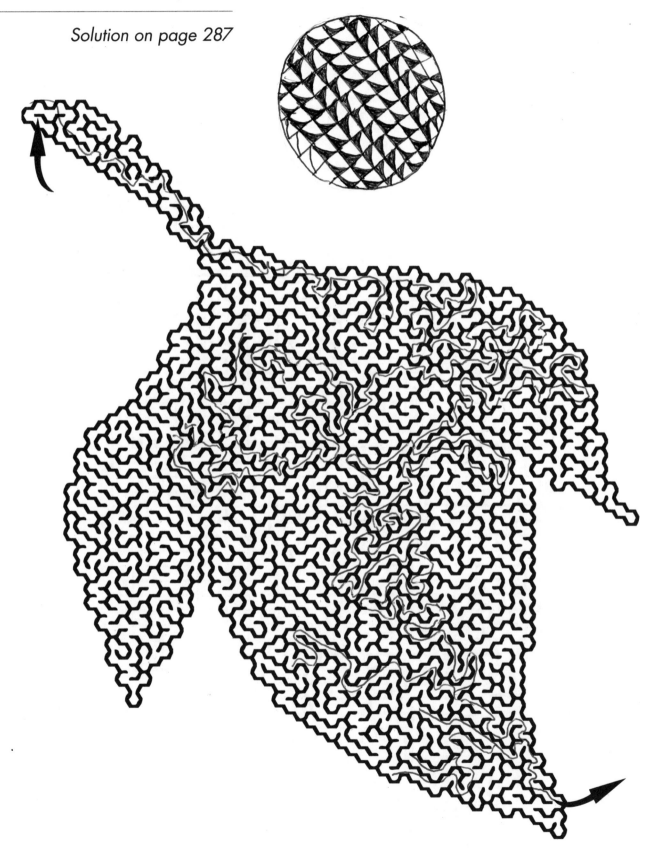

Leaf 6

Solution on page 287

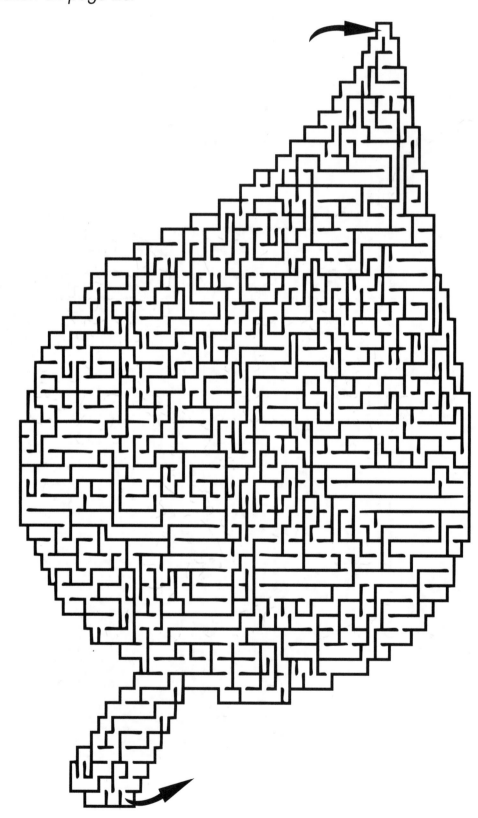

Leaf 7

Solution on page 287

Leaf 8

Solution on page 287

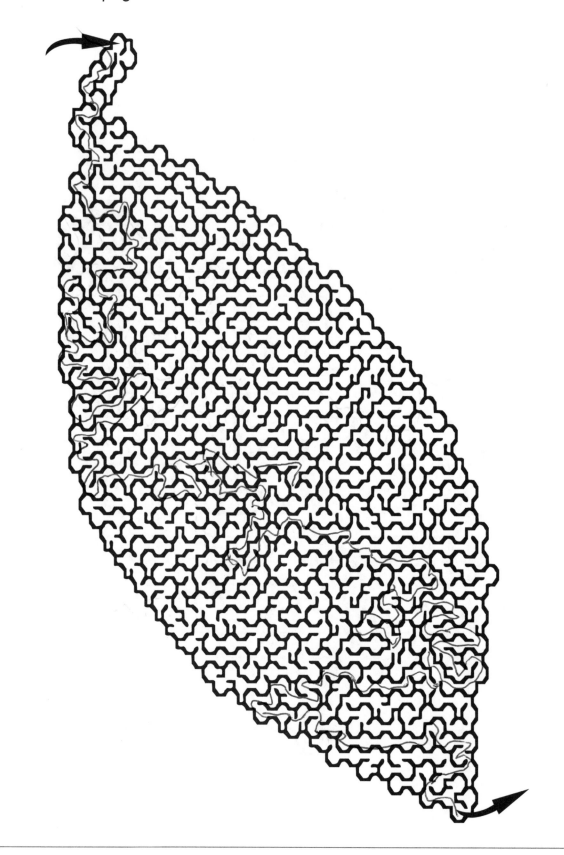

Leaf 9

Solution on page 288

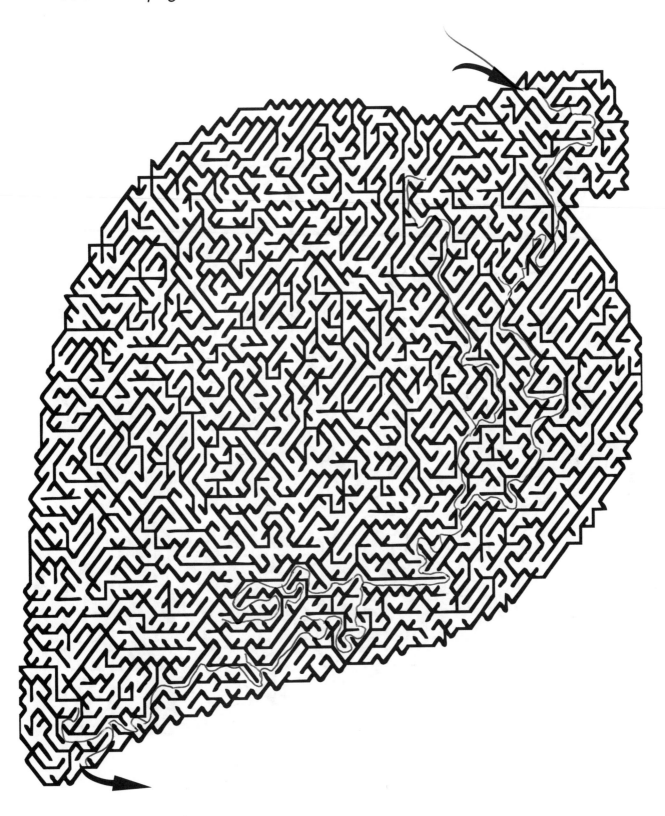

Leaf 10

Solution on page 288

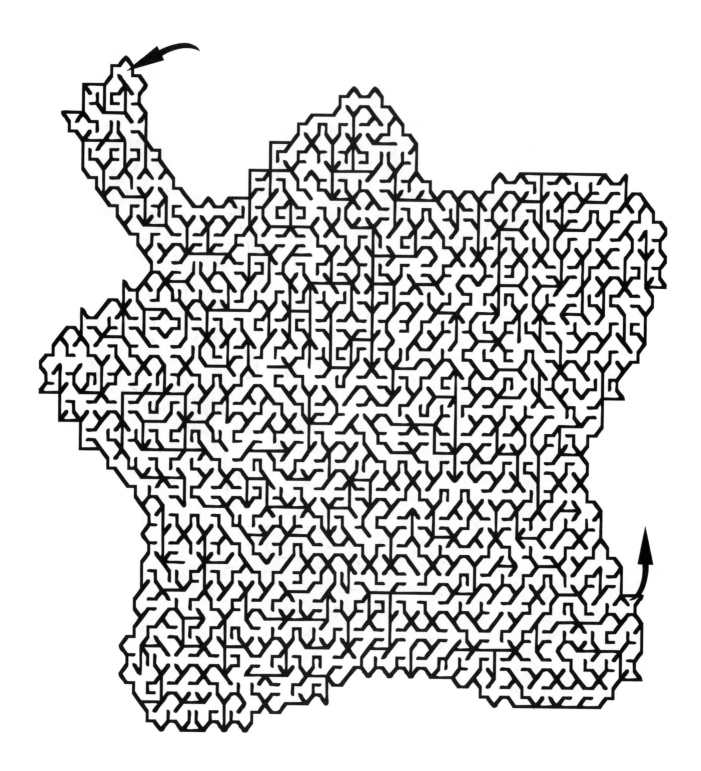

Leaf 11

Solution on page 288

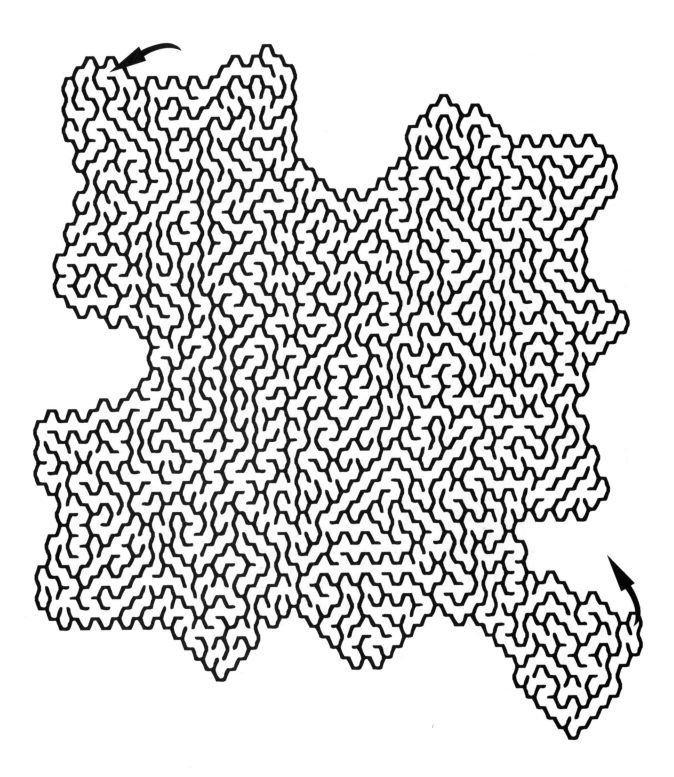

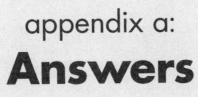

appendix a:
Answers

Chapter 1: Dazzling Diamond Mazes

Diamond 1

Diamond 2

Hourglass 1

Hourglass 2

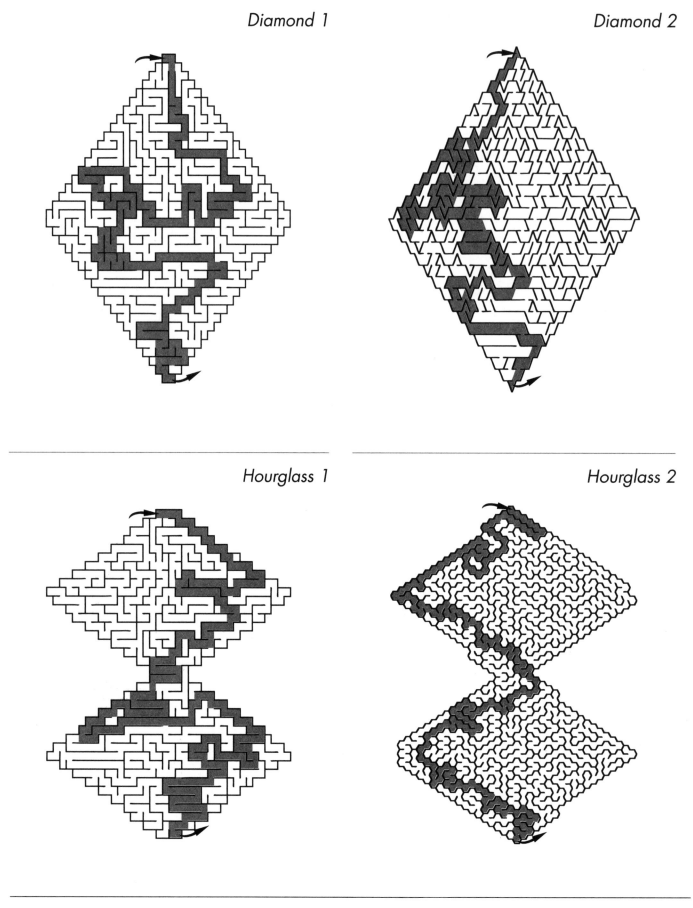

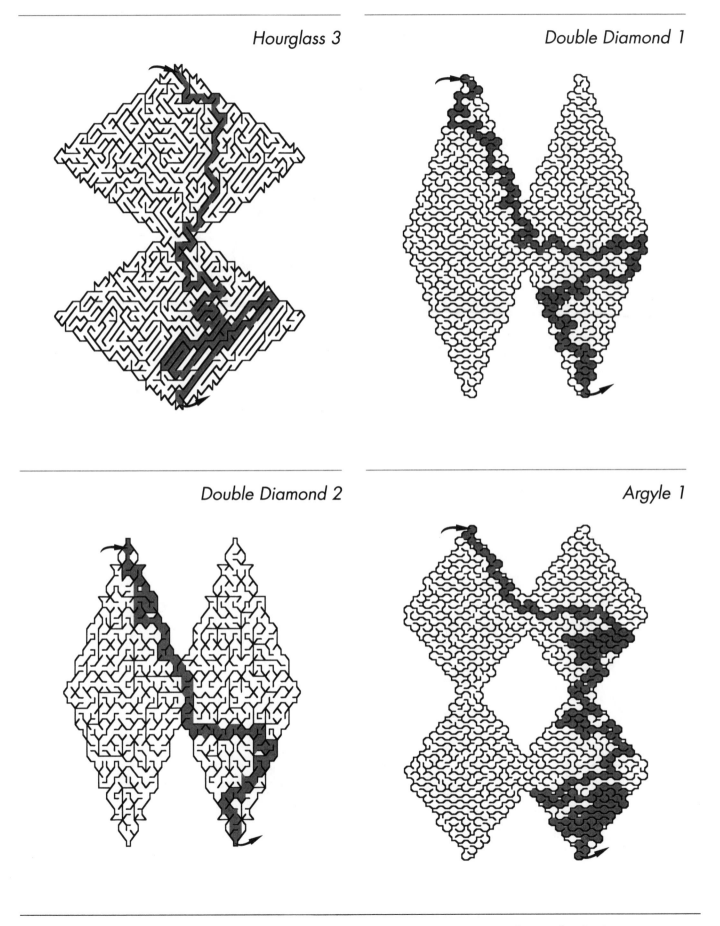

Hourglass 3

Double Diamond 1

Double Diamond 2

Argyle 1

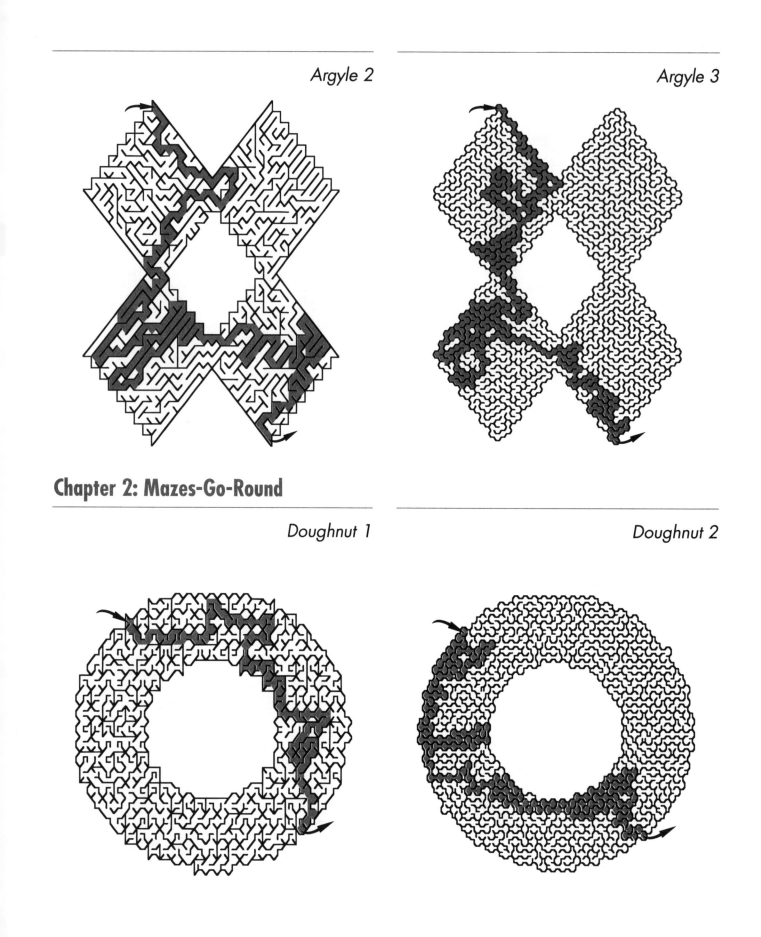

Chapter 2: Mazes-Go-Round

Doughnut 1

Doughnut 2

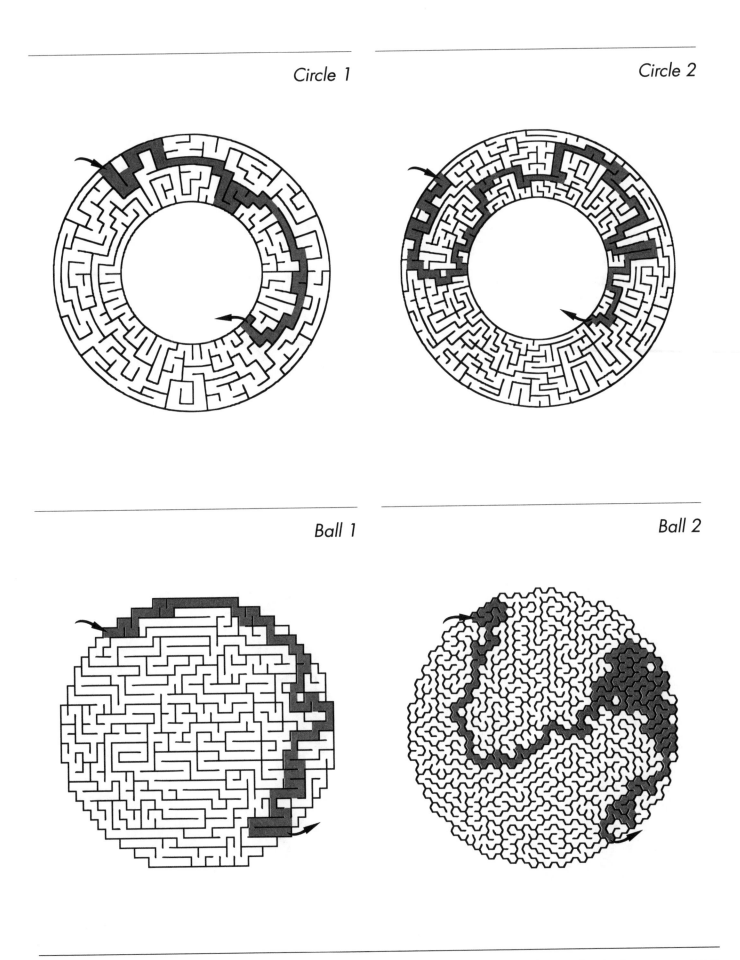

Circle 1

Circle 2

Ball 1

Ball 2

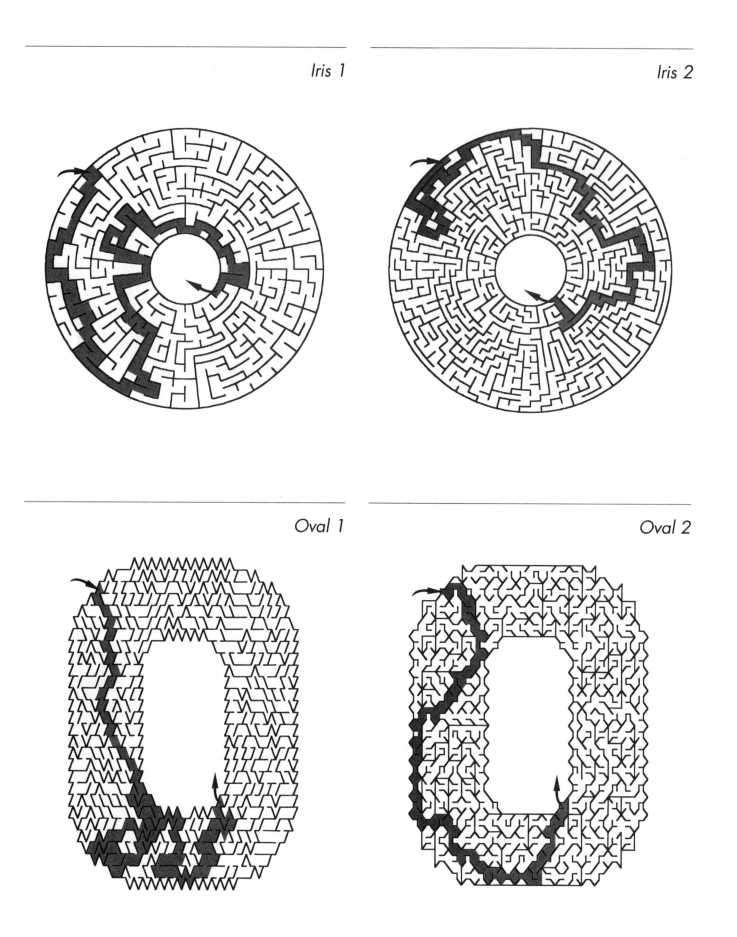

Iris 1

Iris 2

Oval 1

Oval 2

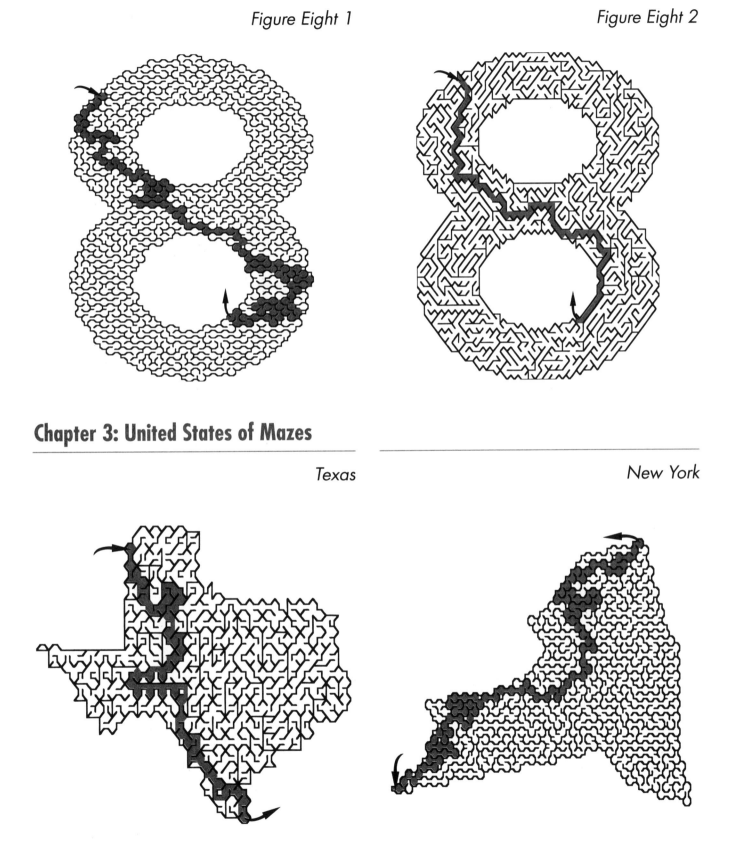

Figure Eight 1

Figure Eight 2

Chapter 3: United States of Mazes

Texas

New York

California

Idaho

Indiana

Maine

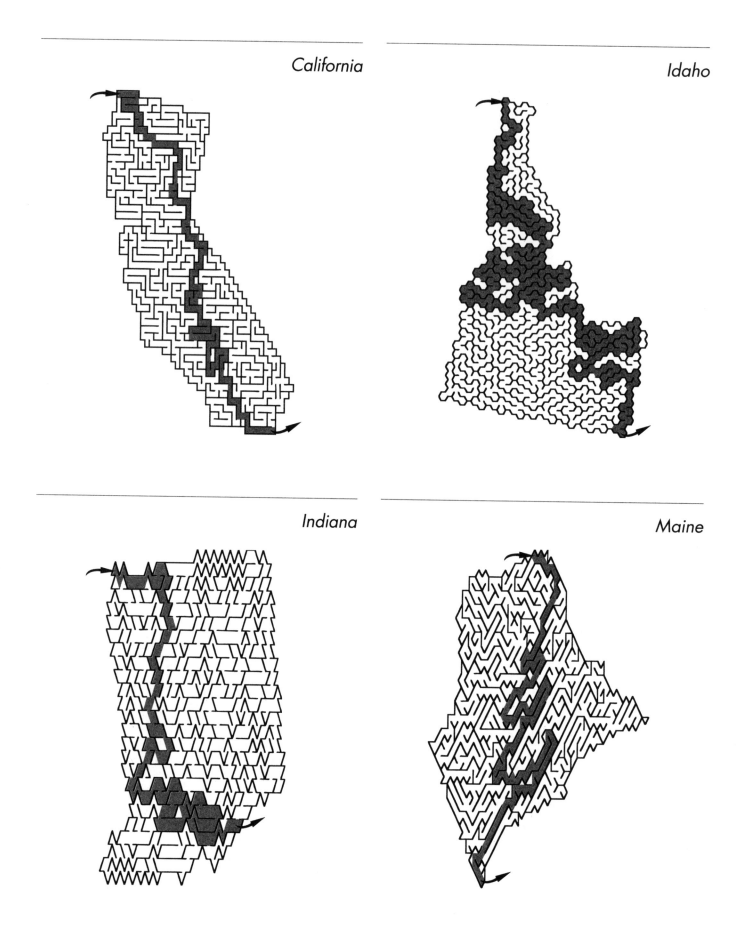

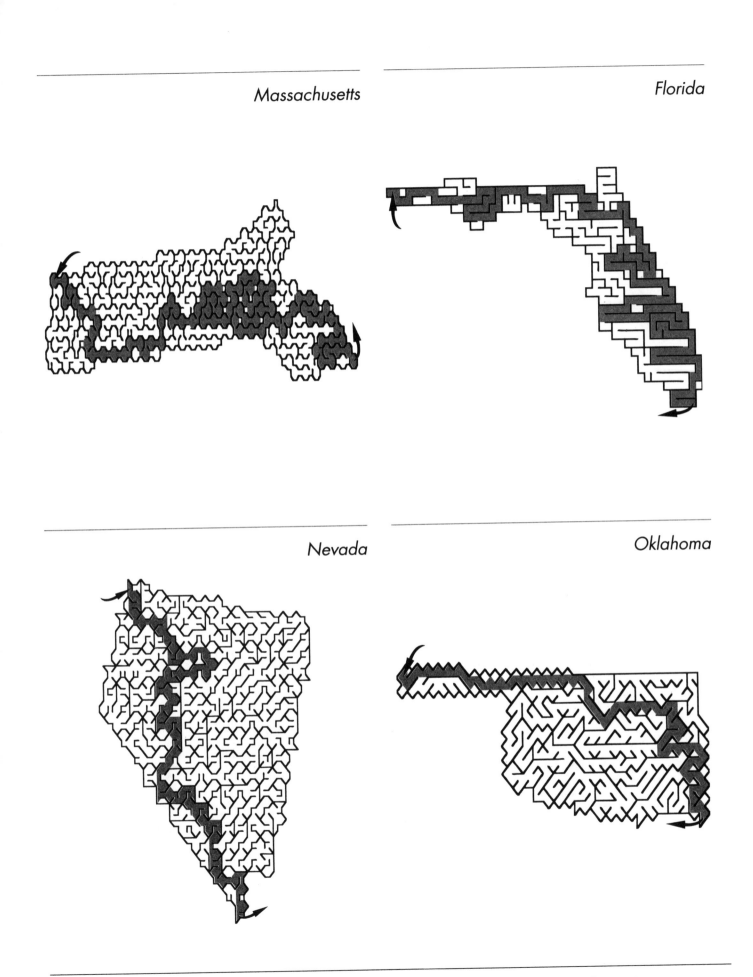

Massachusetts

Florida

Nevada

Oklahoma

Chapter 4: Letter-Perfect Mazes

Letter A

Letter X

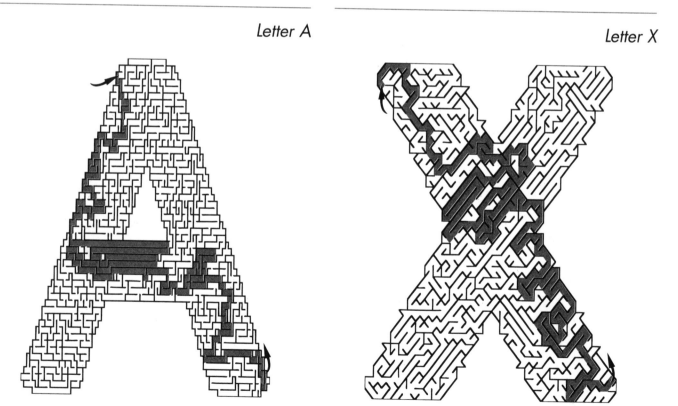

Letter P

Letter R

Letter D

Letter E

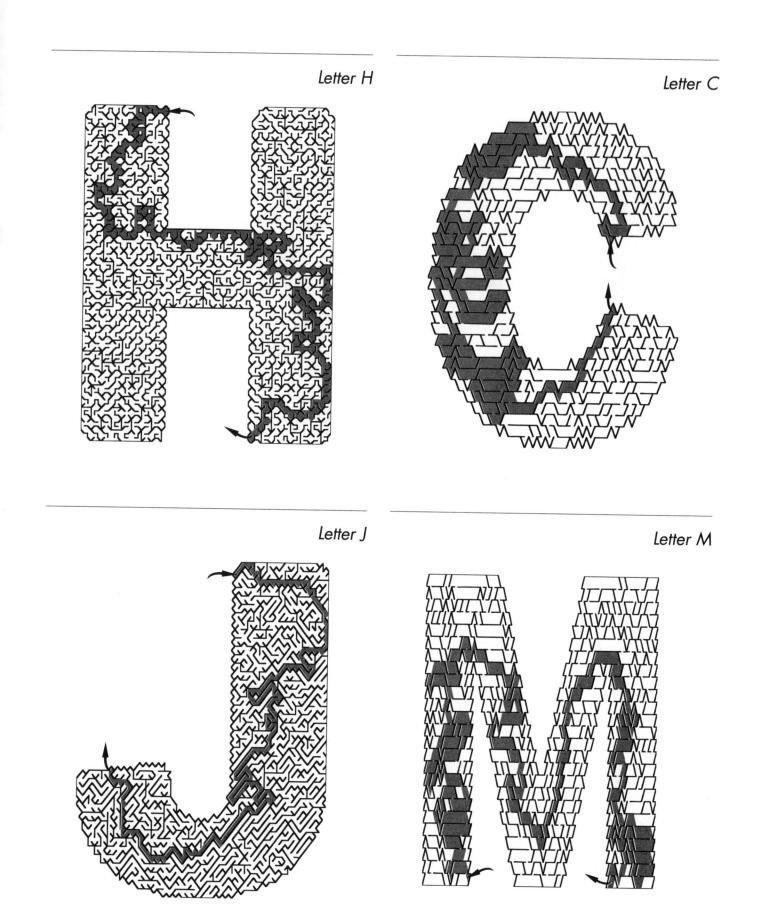

Letter H

Letter C

Letter J

Letter M

Letter Q

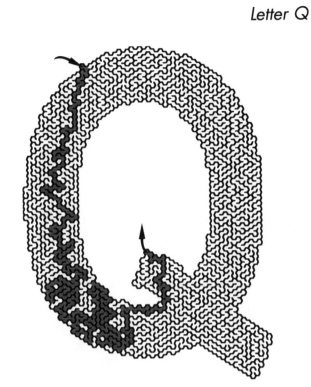

Letter Z

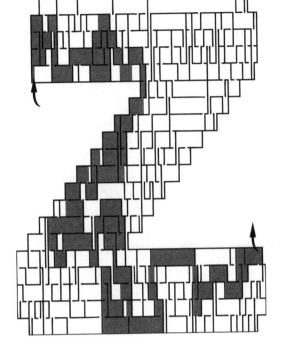

Chapter 5: Be Square Mazes

Full Square

Four Sides

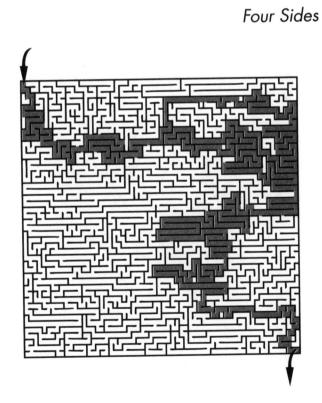

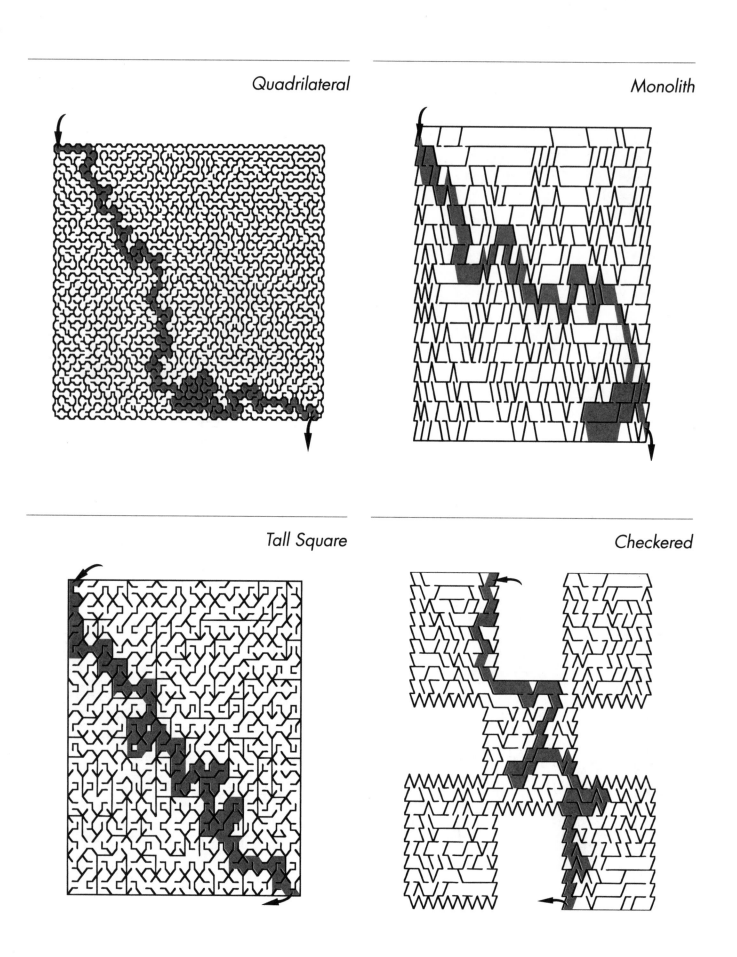

Quadrilateral

Monolith

Tall Square

Checkered

Framed

Square Flower

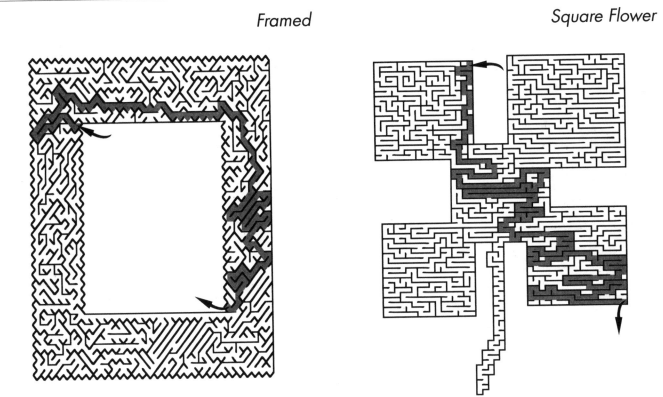

Triple Square

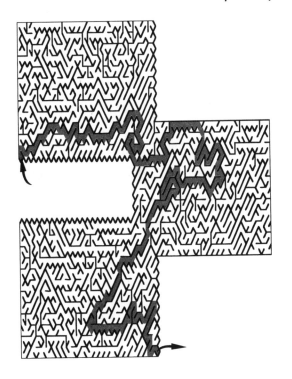

Connected Squares

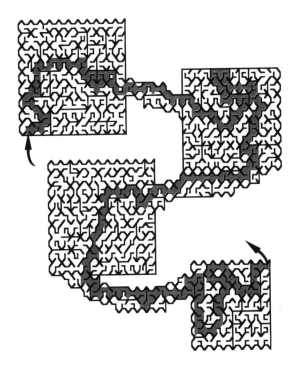

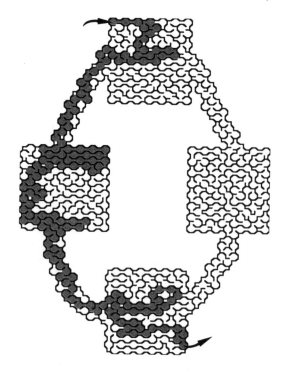

Chapter 6: Mazes for the Holidays

Be My Valentine

Saint Patrick's Day Shamrock

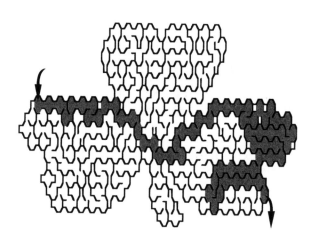

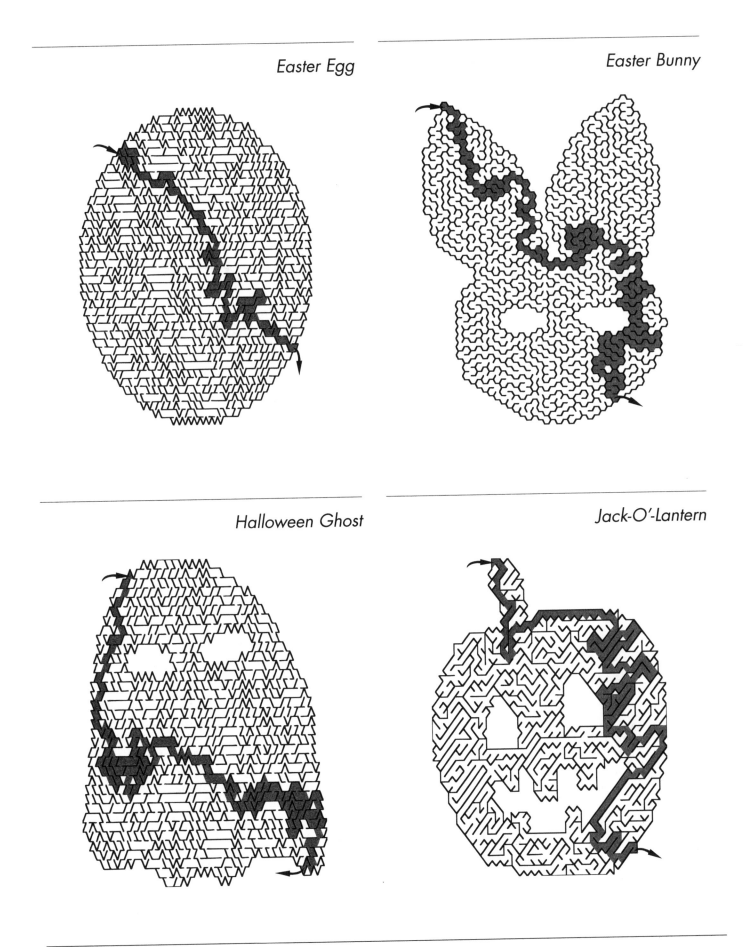

Easter Egg

Easter Bunny

Halloween Ghost

Jack-O'-Lantern

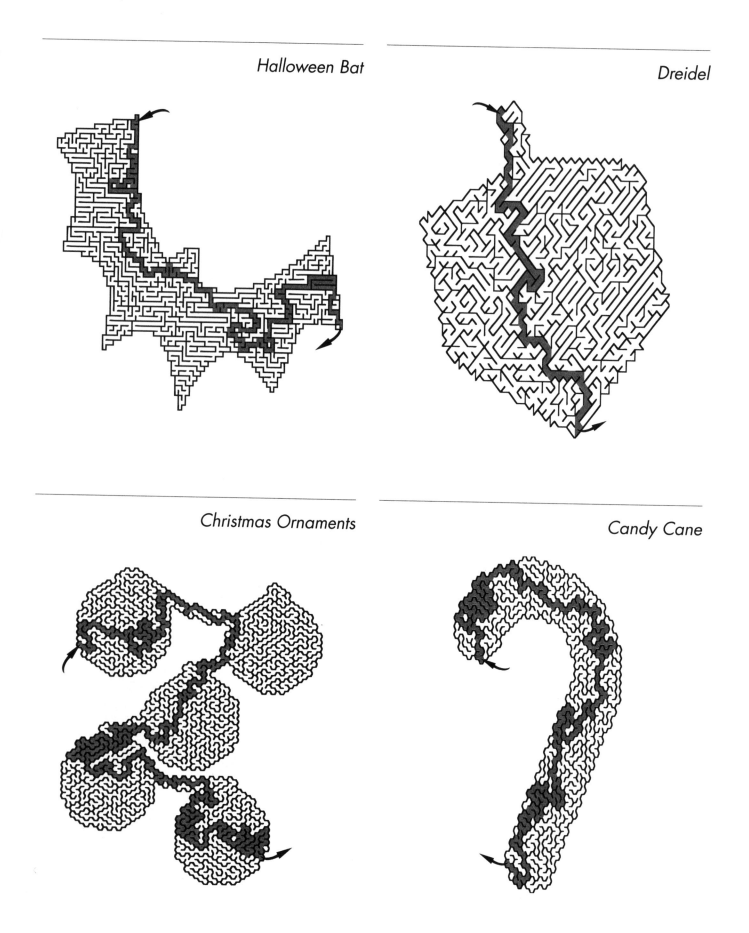

Halloween Bat

Dreidel

Christmas Ornaments

Candy Cane

Christmas Tree

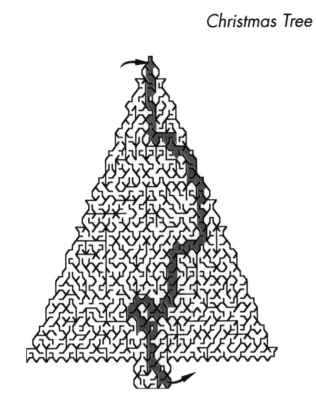

Chapter 7: Mazes Take Off!

Space Pod

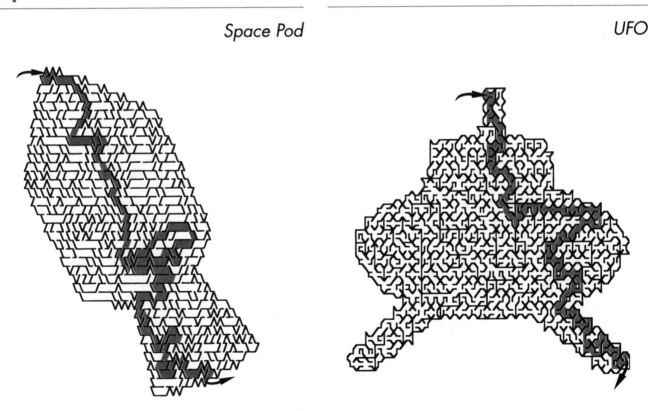

UFO

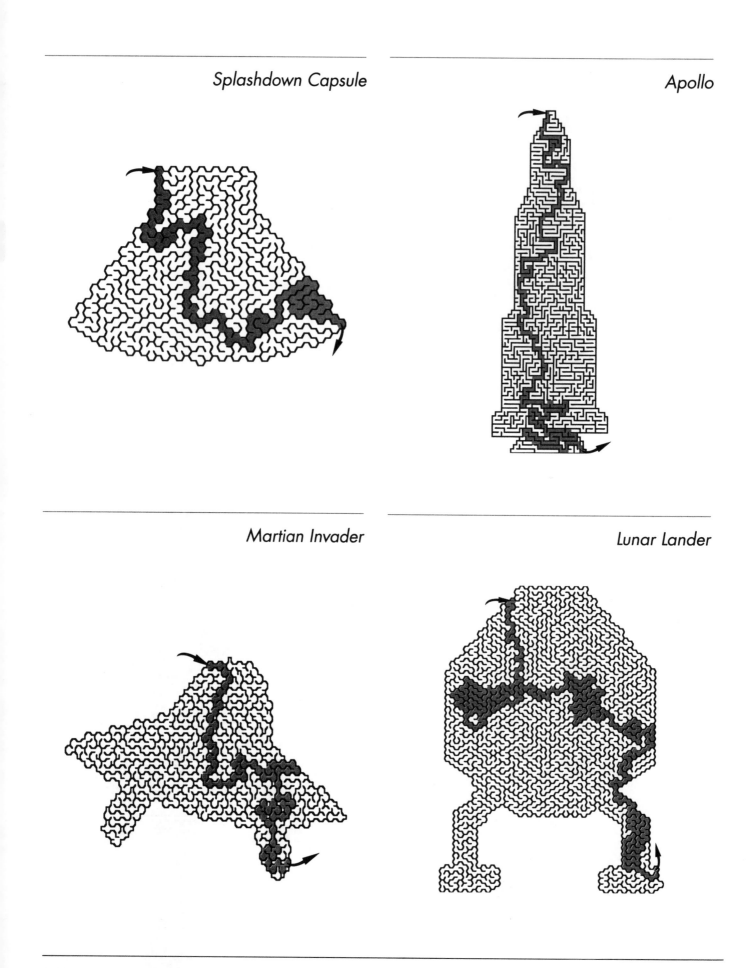

Splashdown Capsule

Apollo

Martian Invader

Lunar Lander

Space Shuttle

Chapter 8: No Place Like Home Mazes

Lighthouse

City Homes

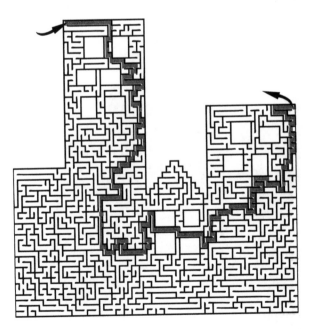

Barn

Igloo

Dog House

Teepee

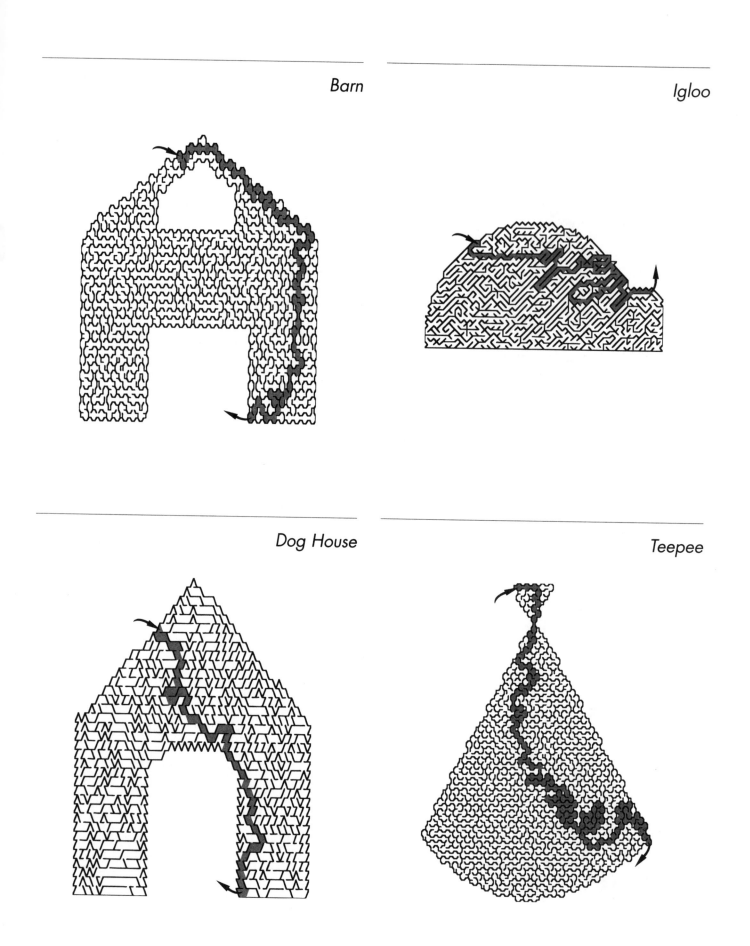

Bird House

Hut

Townhouse

A-Frame

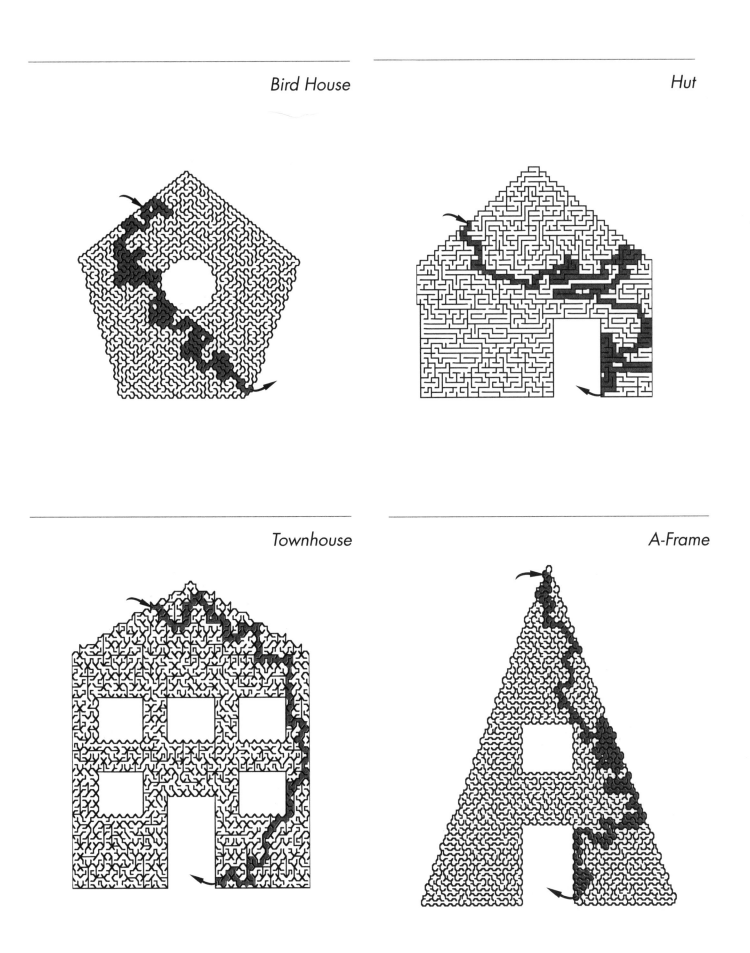

Cheerful

Big Laugh

Toothy

Smile

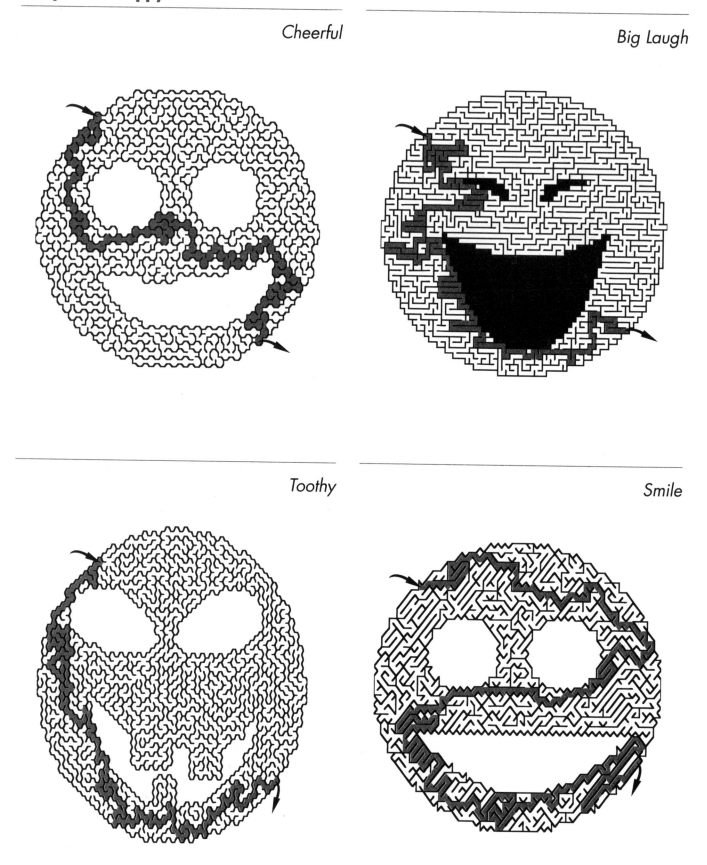

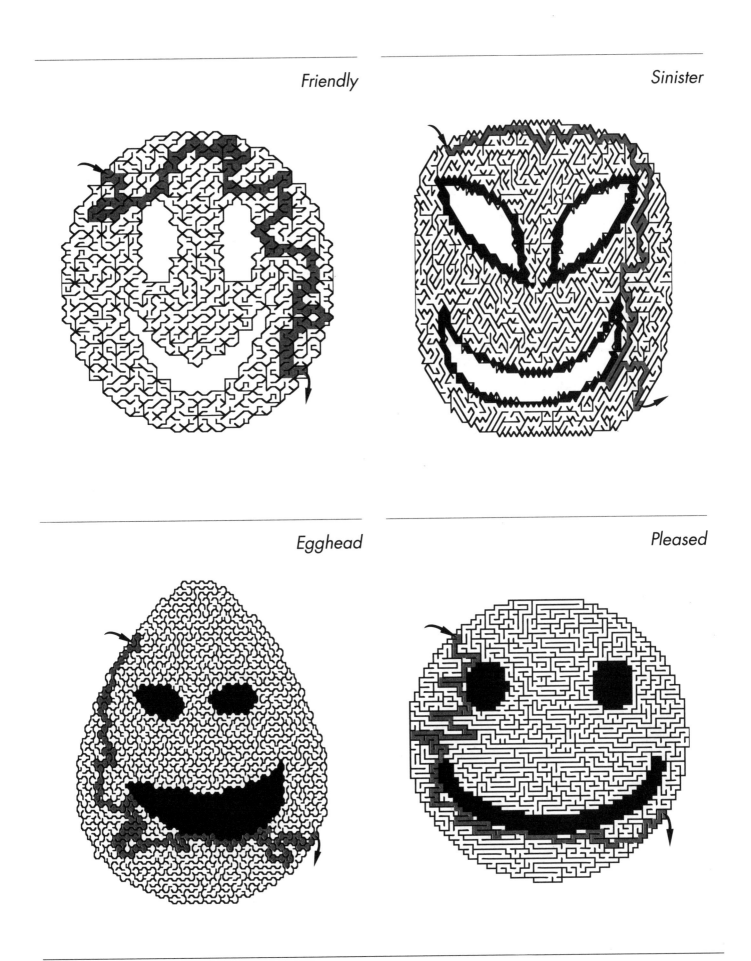

Friendly

Sinister

Egghead

Pleased

Chapter 10: Mazes By The Numbers

Zero

One

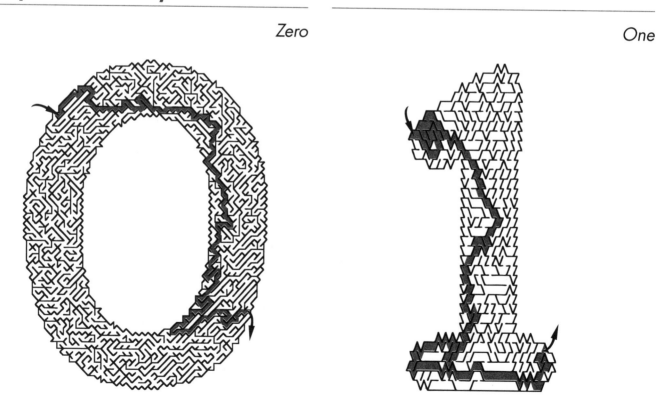

Two

Three

Four

Five

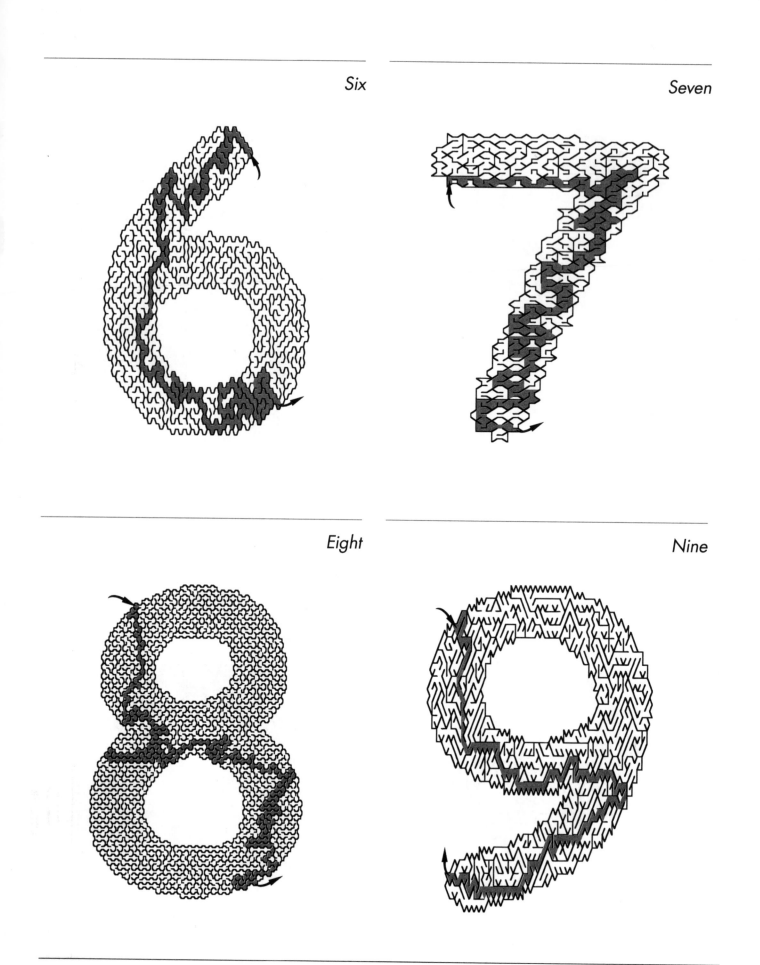

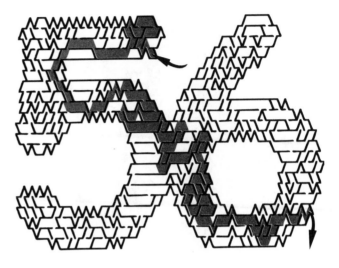

Chapter 11: Star-Struck Mazes

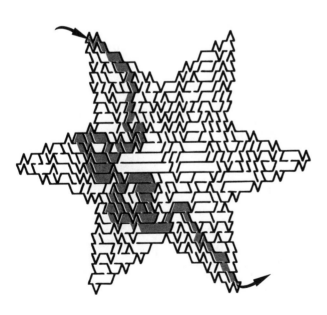

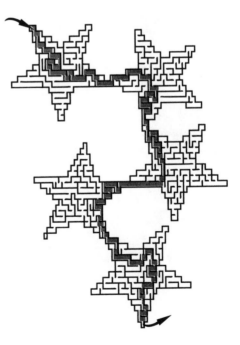

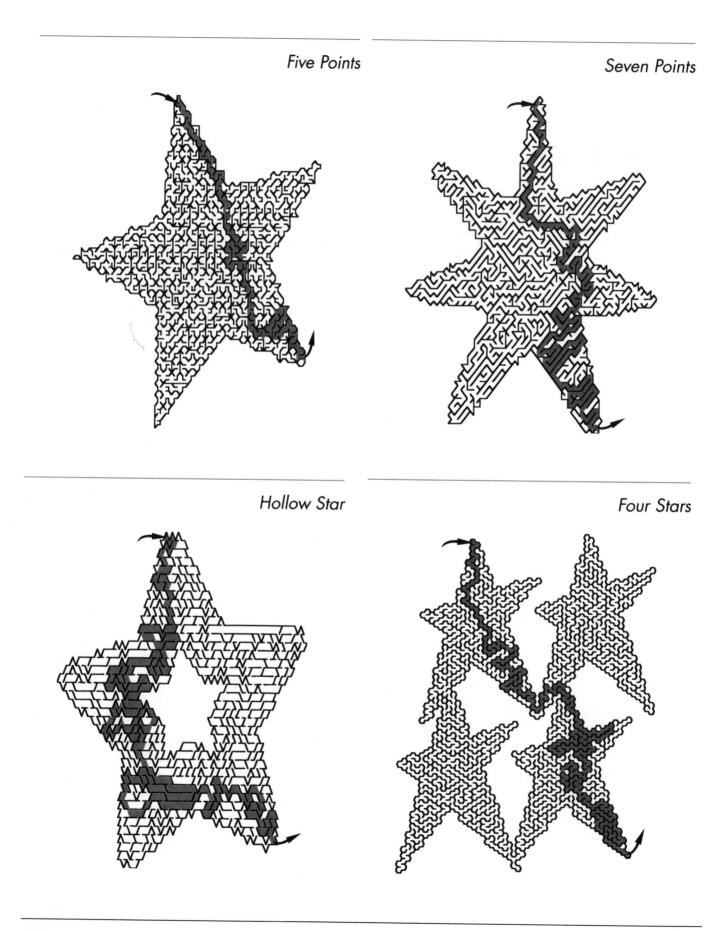

Five Points

Seven Points

Hollow Star

Four Stars

Designer Star

Pointy Star

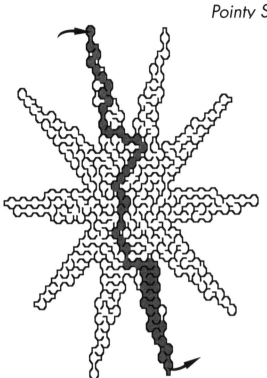

Chapter 12: Butterfly Mazes

Sea Star

Butterfly 1

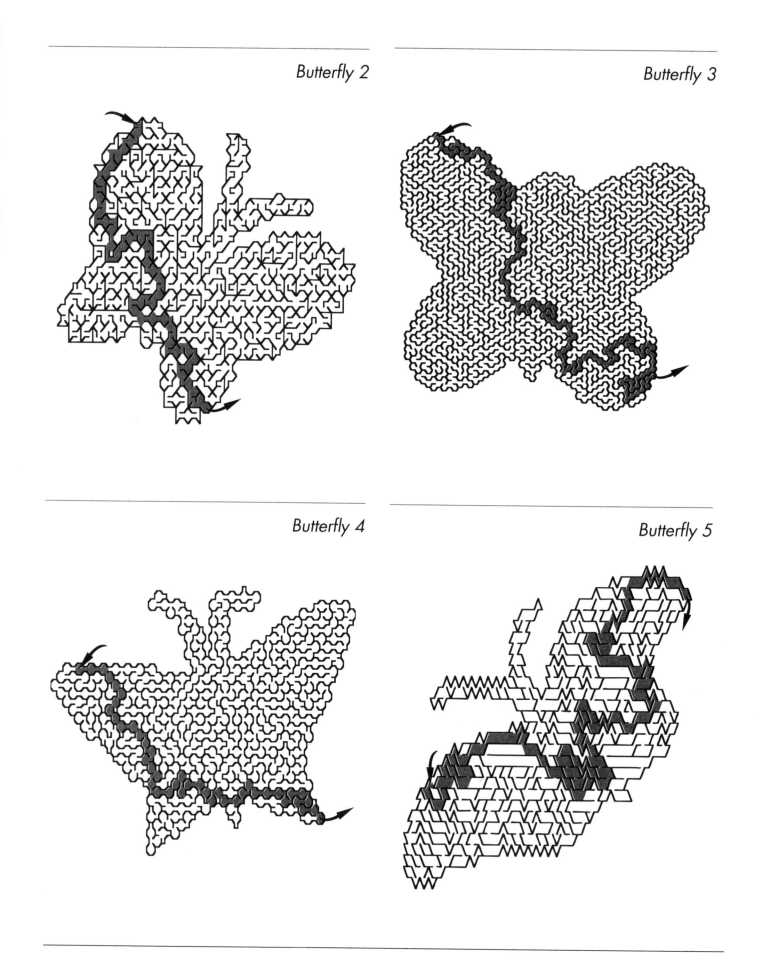

Butterfly 2

Butterfly 3

Butterfly 4

Butterfly 5

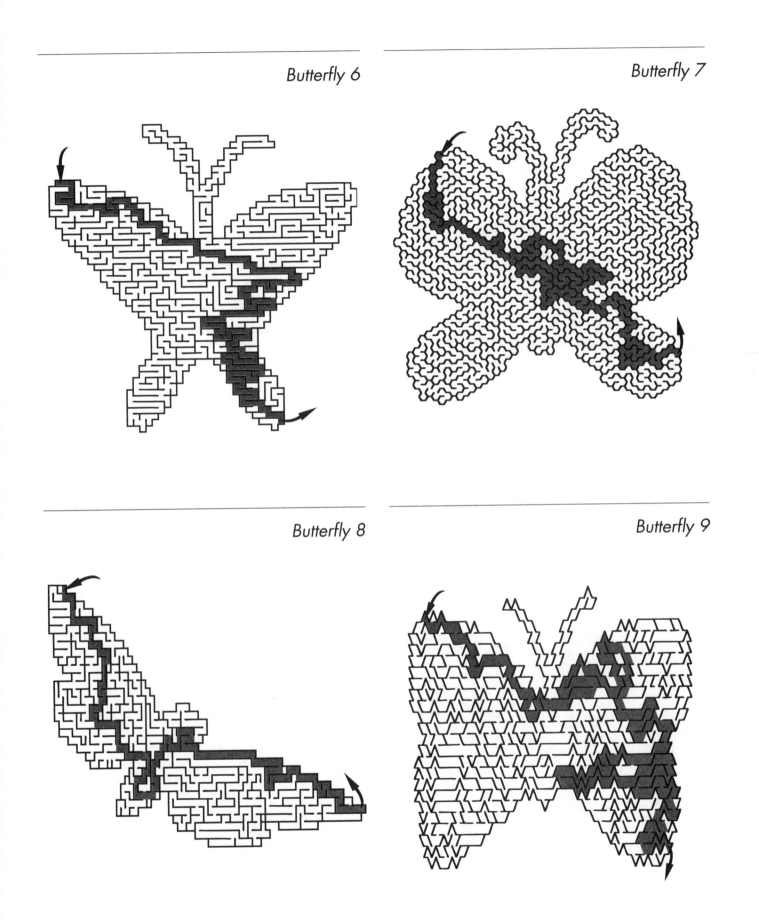

Butterfly 6

Butterfly 7

Butterfly 8

Butterfly 9

Chapter 13: Blockhead Mazes

Big Nose

Shades

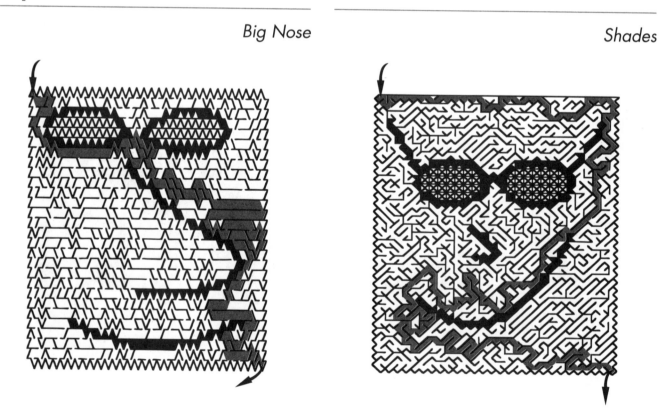

Robot

Big Smile

Devious

Big Mouth

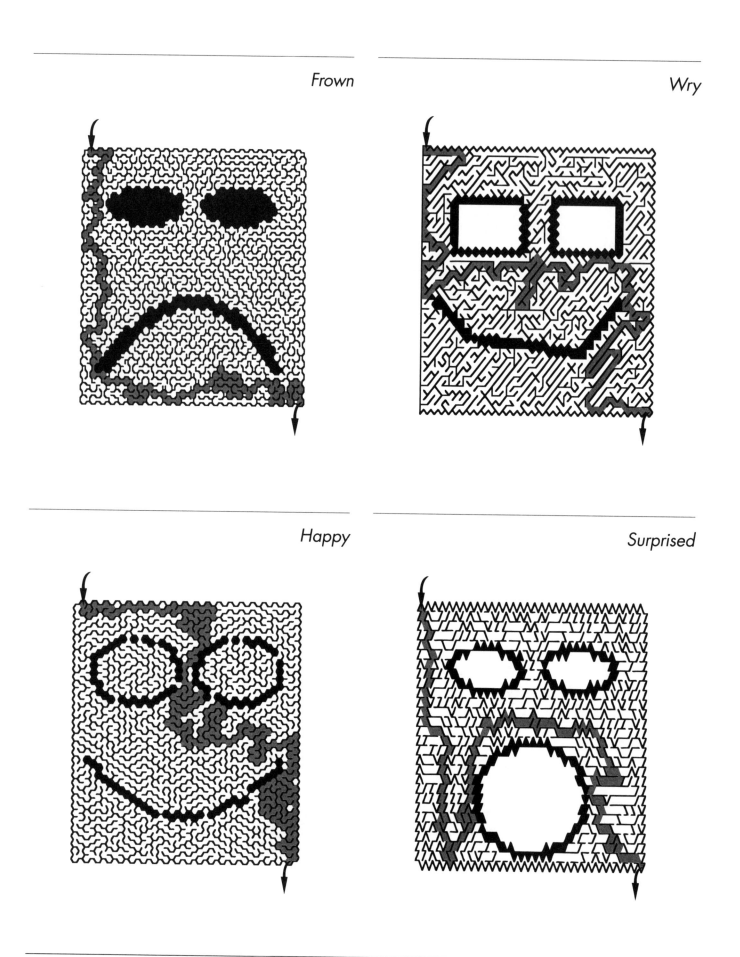

Frown

Wry

Happy

Surprised

Flower 1

Flower 2

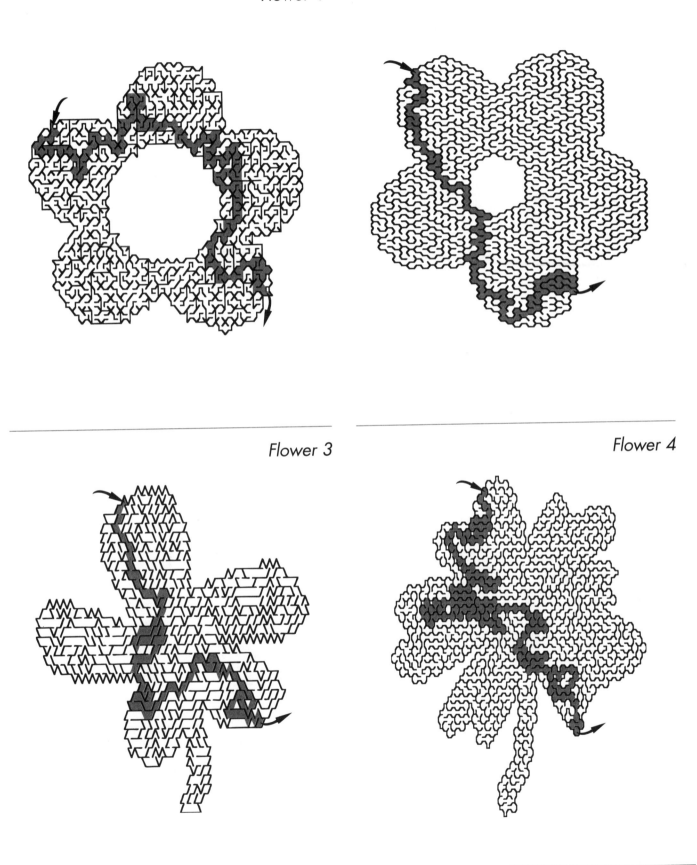

Flower 3

Flower 4

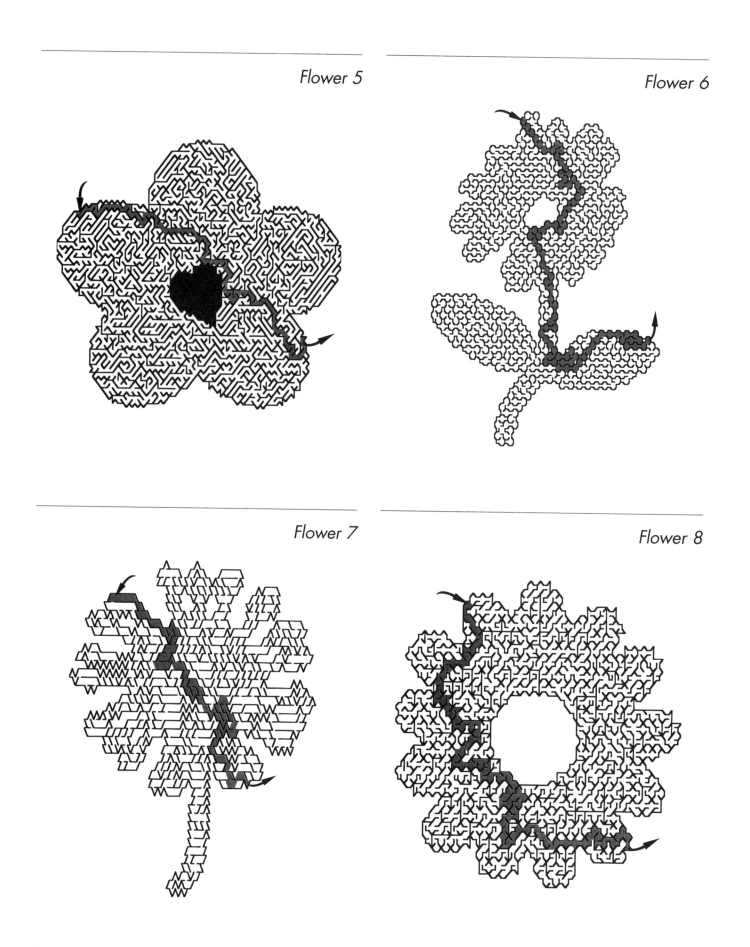

Flower 5

Flower 6

Flower 7

Flower 8

Flower 9

Flower 10

Chapter 15: Bubble Mazes

Bubbles 1

Bubbles 2

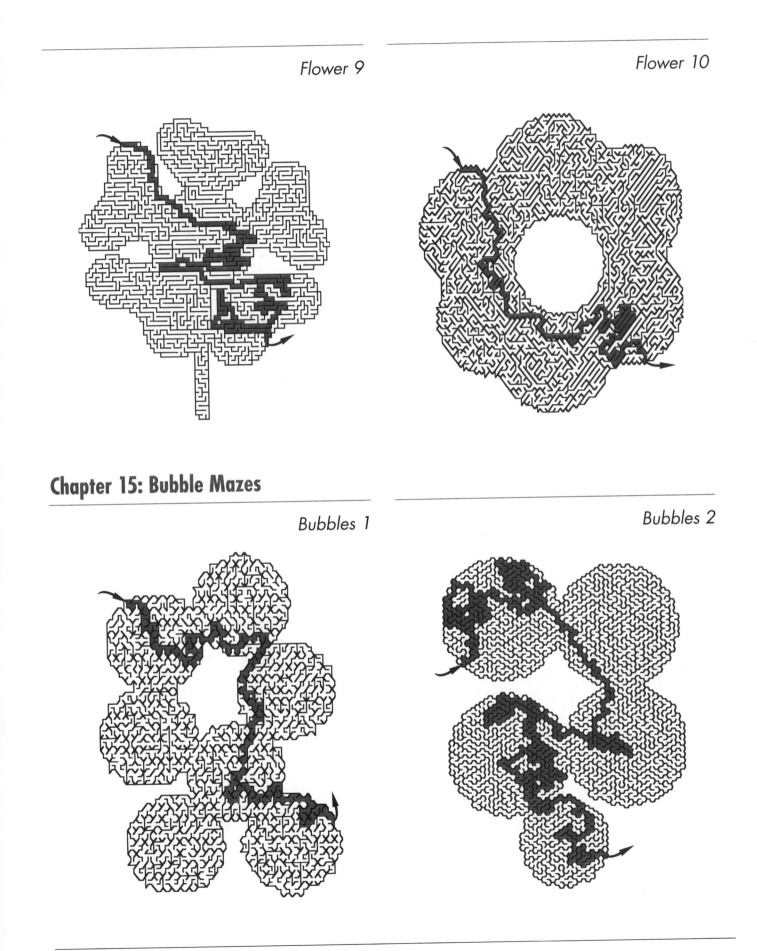

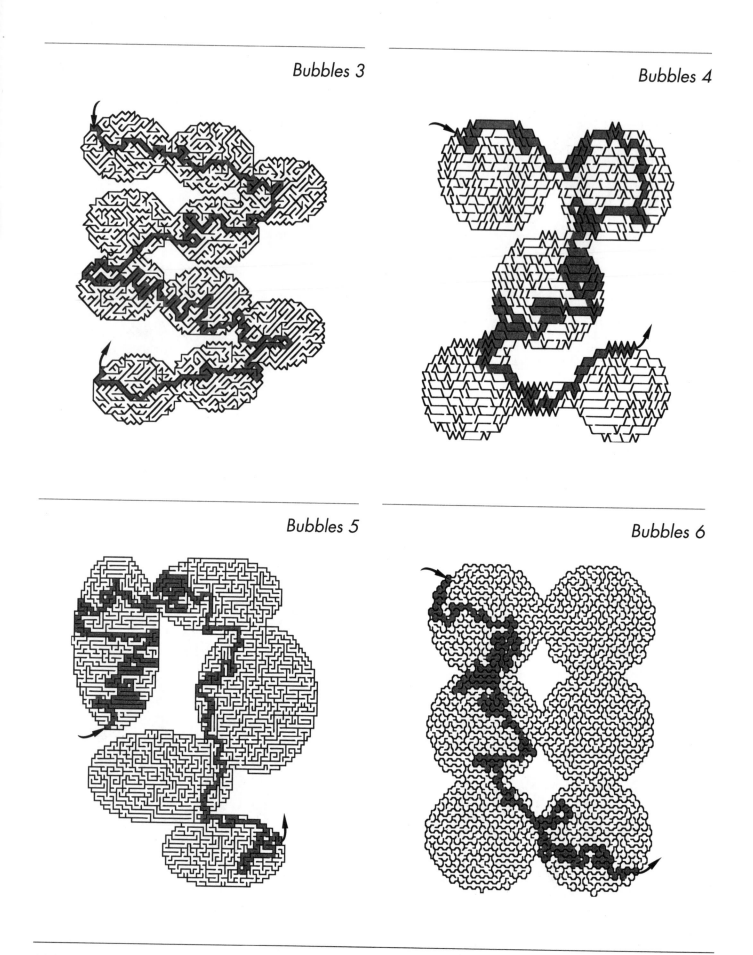

Bubbles 3

Bubbles 4

Bubbles 5

Bubbles 6

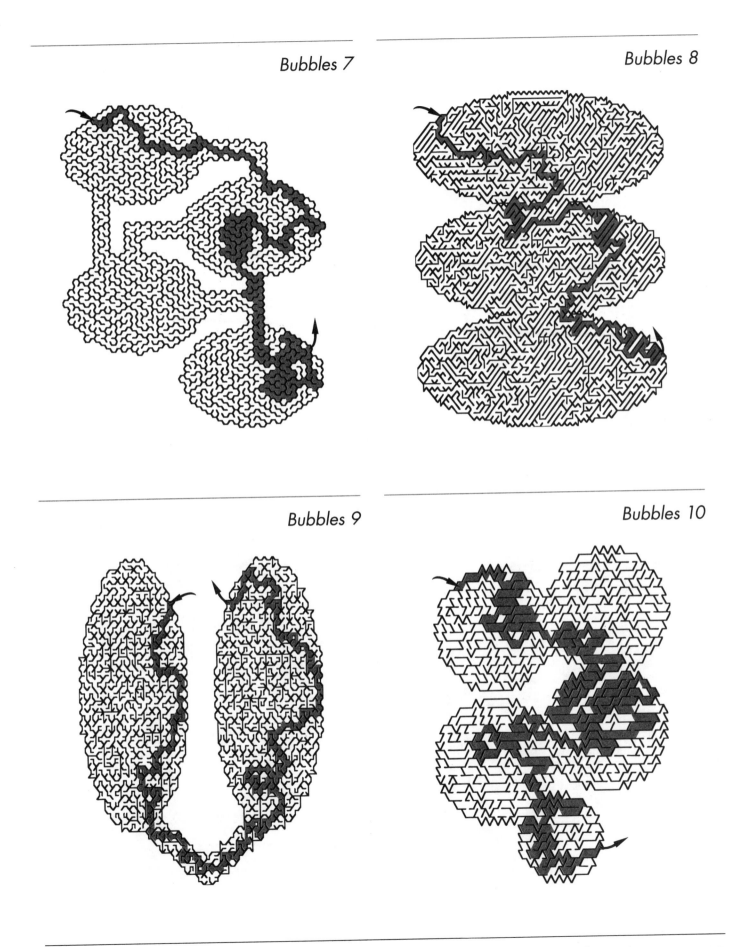

Bubbles 7

Bubbles 8

Bubbles 9

Bubbles 10

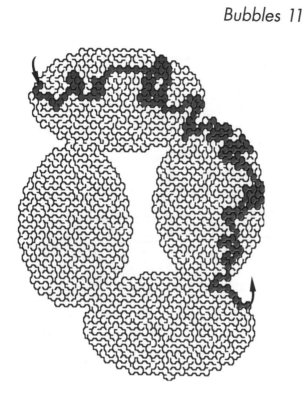

Chapter 16: Blueprint Mazes

Blueprint 1

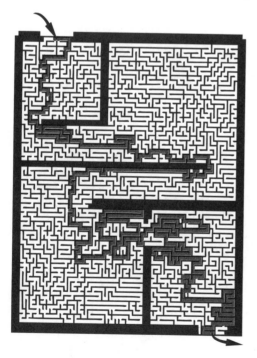

Blueprint 2

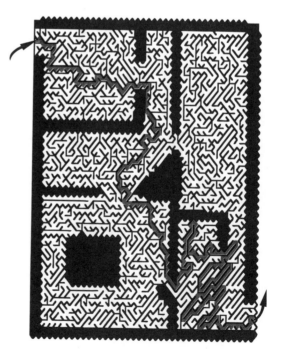

Blueprint 3

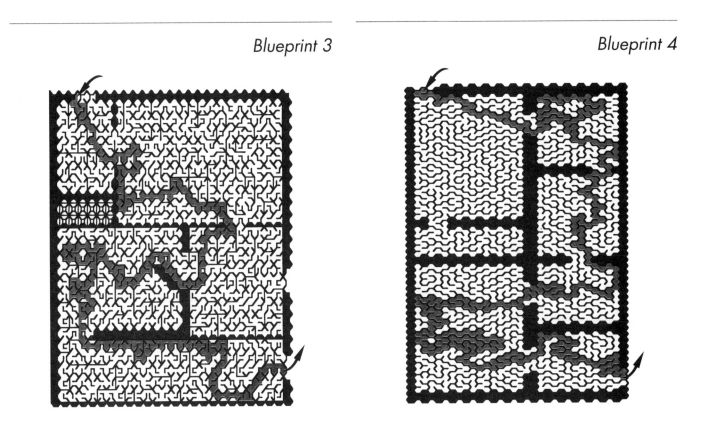

Blueprint 4

Blueprint 5

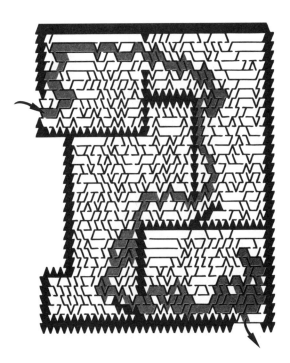

Blueprint 6

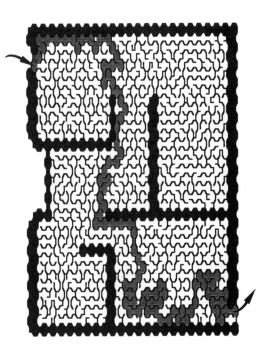

Blueprint 7

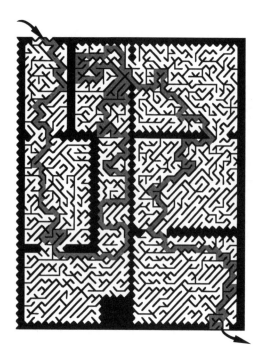

Blueprint 8

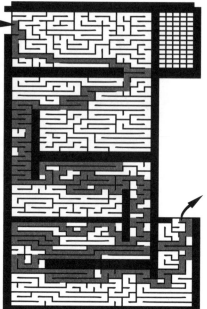

Blueprint 9

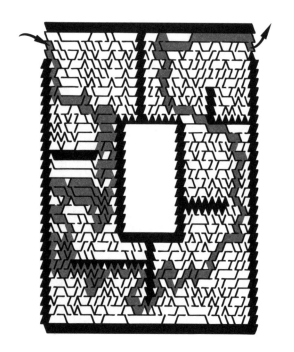

Blueprint 10

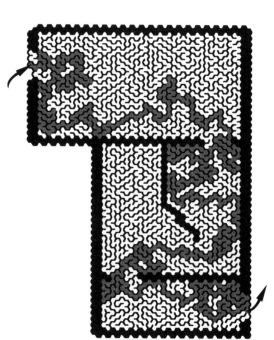

Chapter 17: Cups Full of Mazes

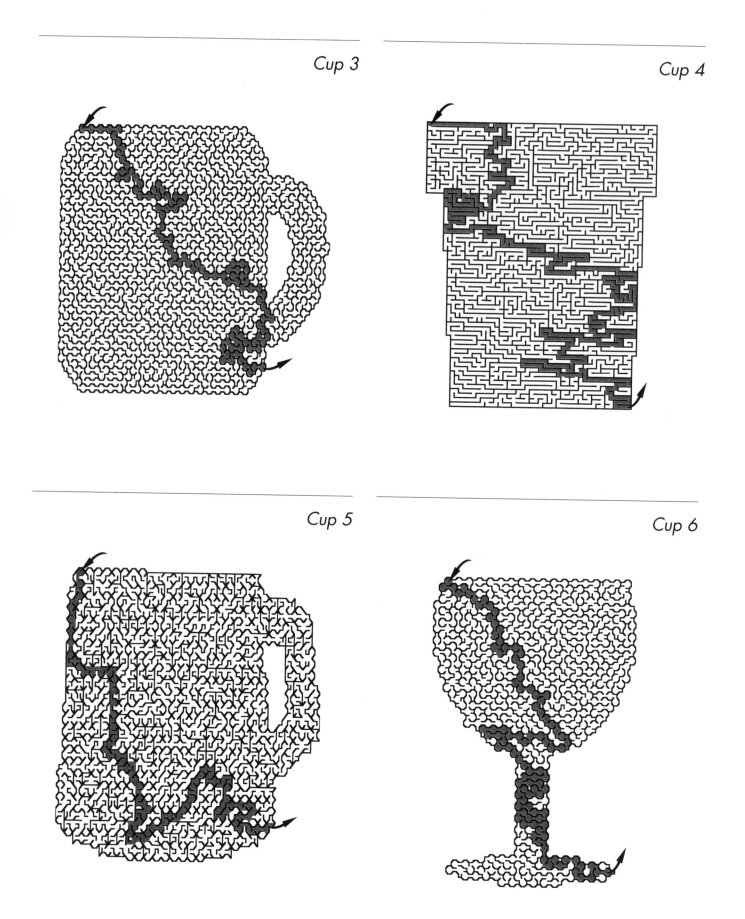

Cup 3

Cup 4

Cup 5

Cup 6

Cup 7

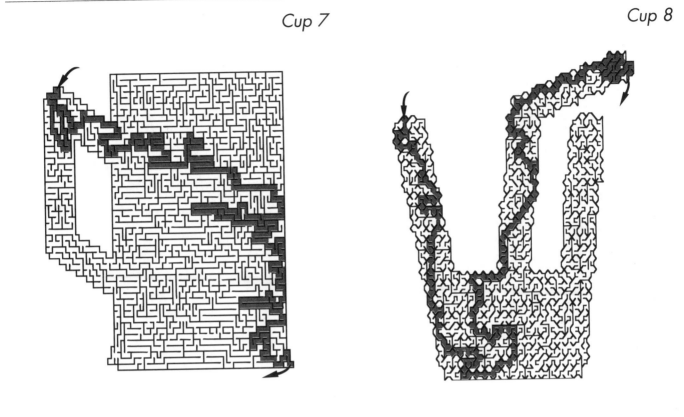

Cup 8

Cup 9

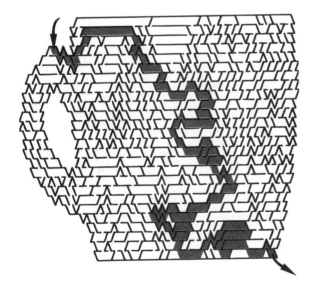

Arrowhead 1

Arrowhead 2

Arrowhead 3

Arrowhead 4

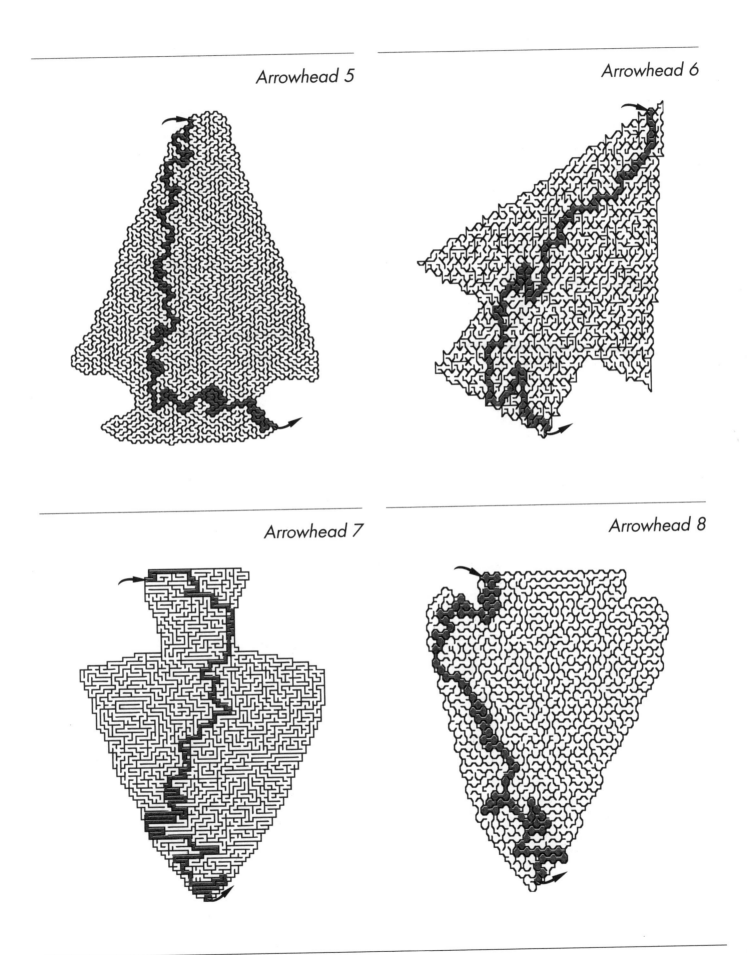

Arrowhead 5

Arrowhead 6

Arrowhead 7

Arrowhead 8

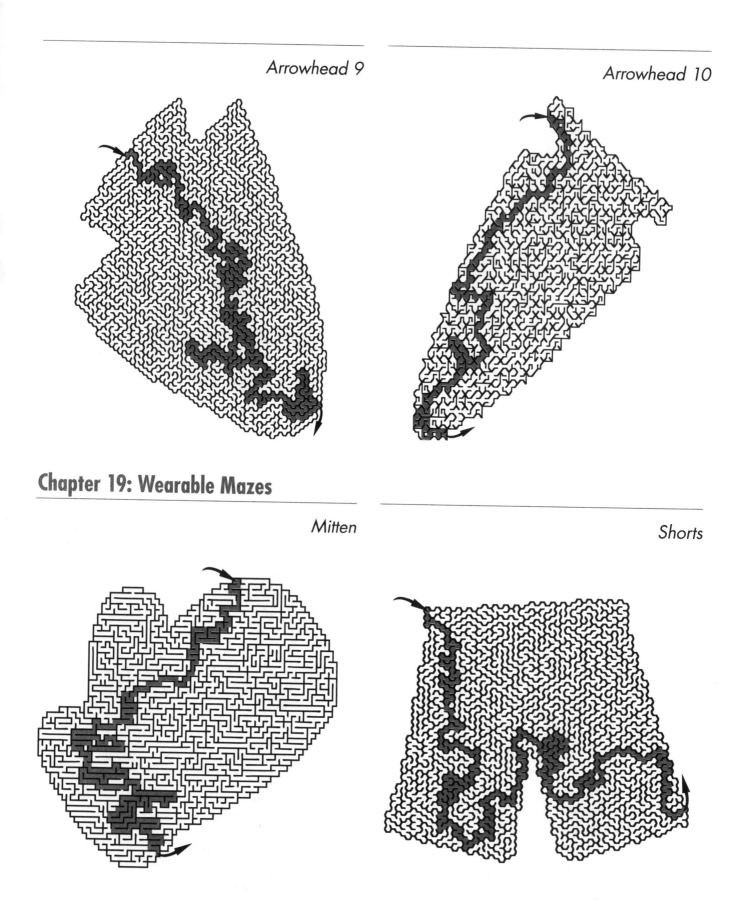

Arrowhead 9

Arrowhead 10

Chapter 19: Wearable Mazes

Mitten

Shorts

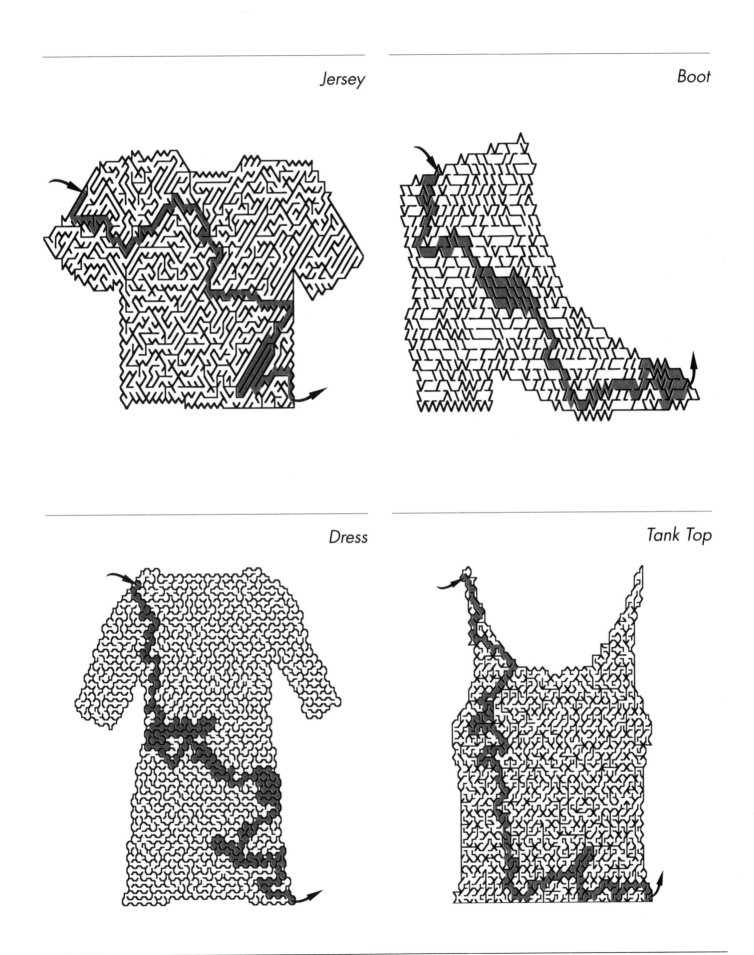

Jersey

Boot

Dress

Tank Top

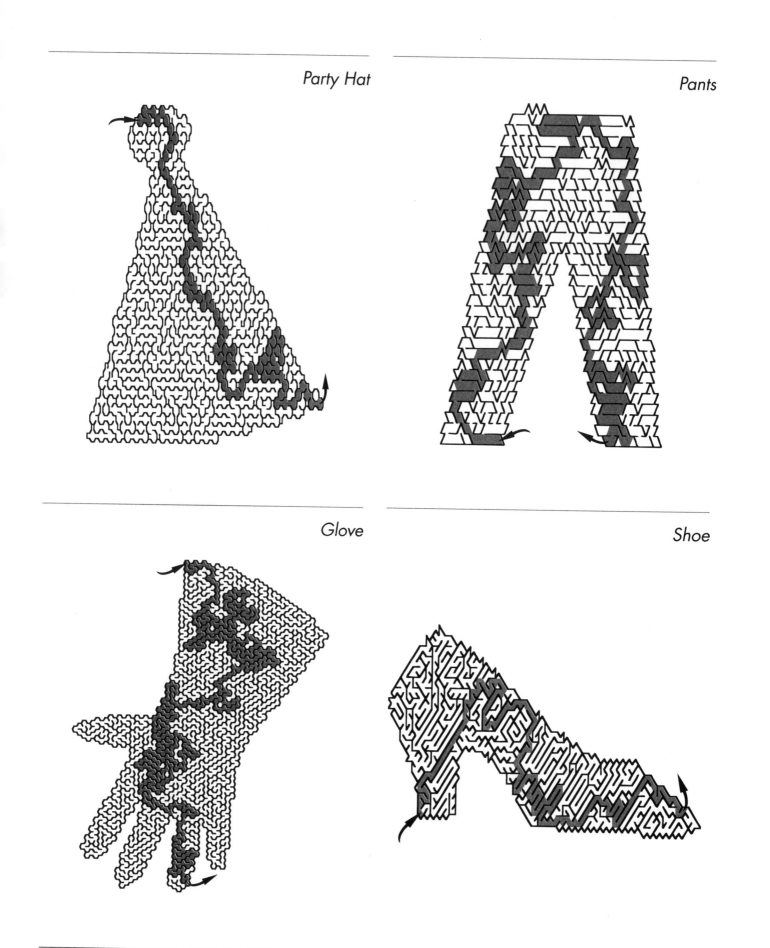

Party Hat

Pants

Glove

Shoe

Shirt

Fish 1

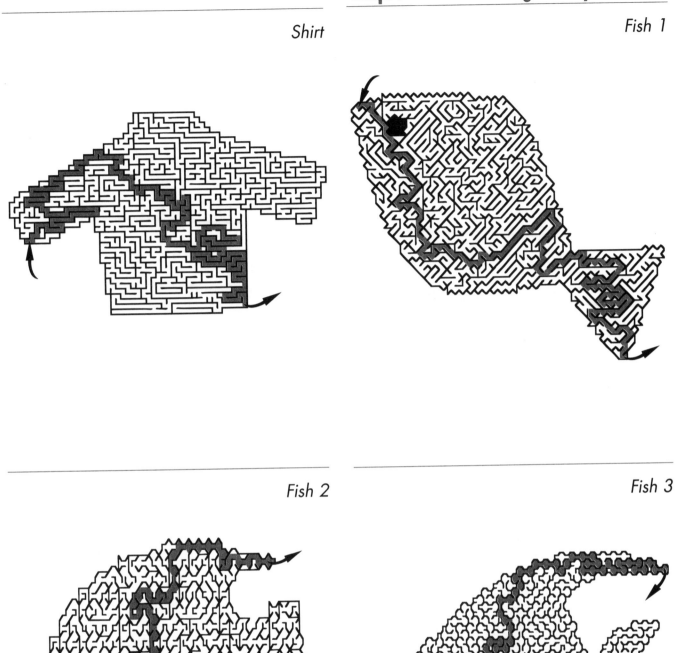

Fish 2

Fish 3

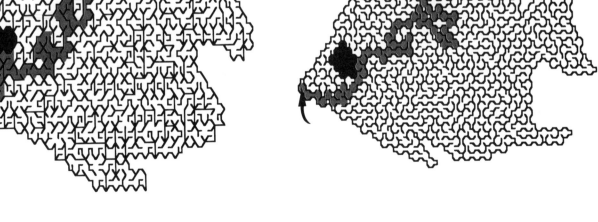

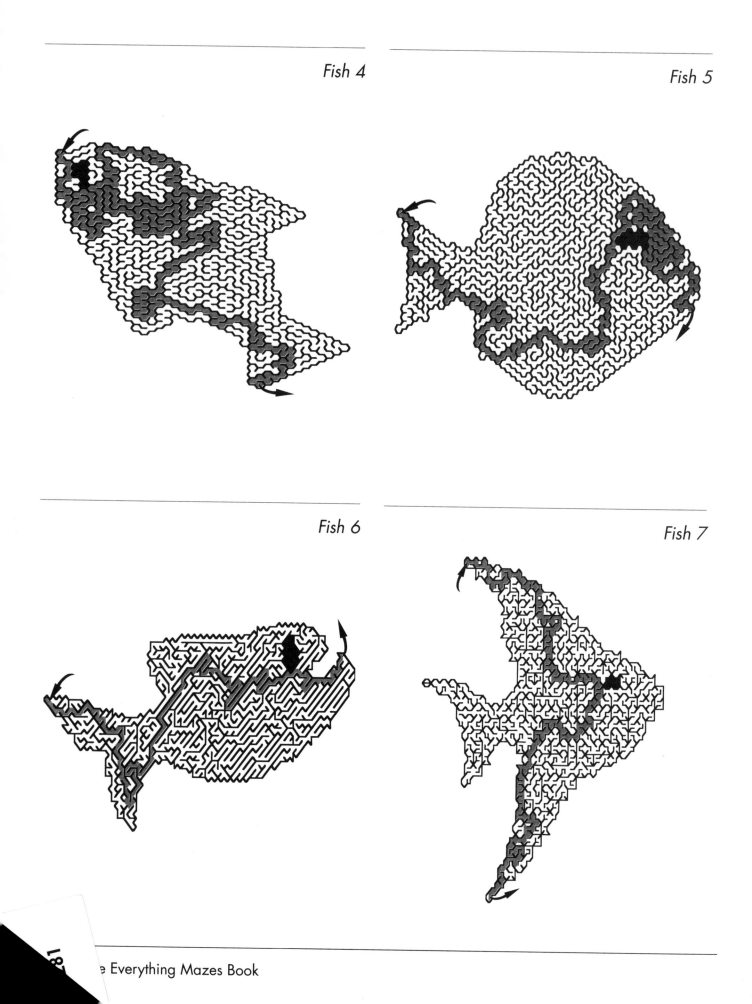

Fish 4

Fish 5

Fish 6

Fish 7

e Everything Mazes Book

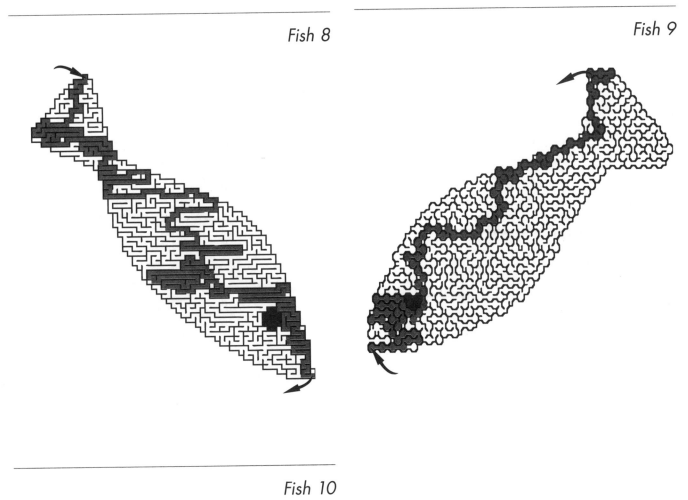

Fish 8

Fish 9

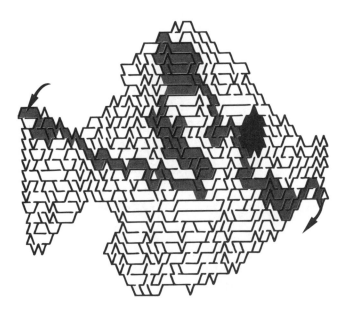

Fish 10

Pyramid 1

Pyramid 2

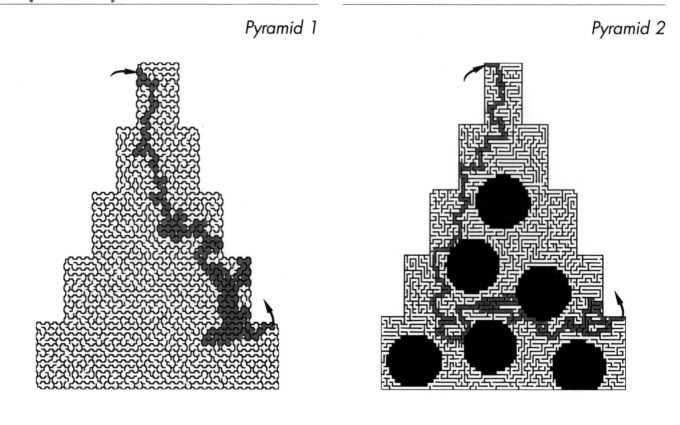

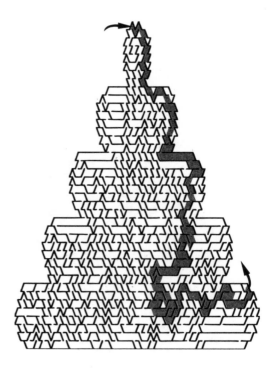

Pyramid 3

Pyramid 4

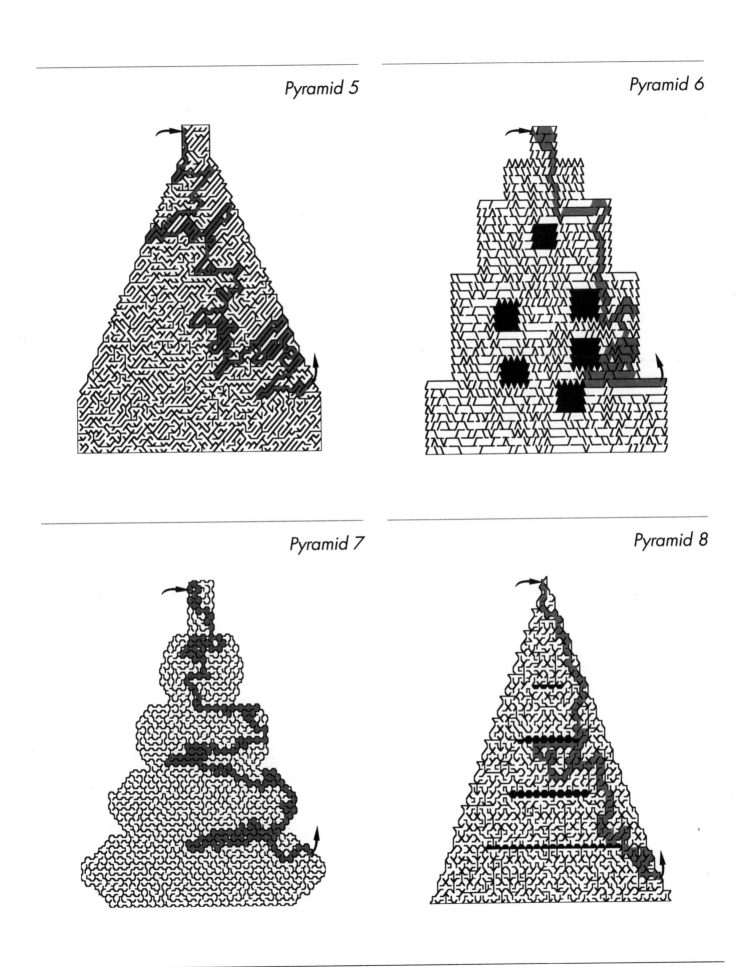

Pyramid 5

Pyramid 6

Pyramid 7

Pyramid 8

Leaf 1

Leaf 2

Leaf 3

Leaf 4

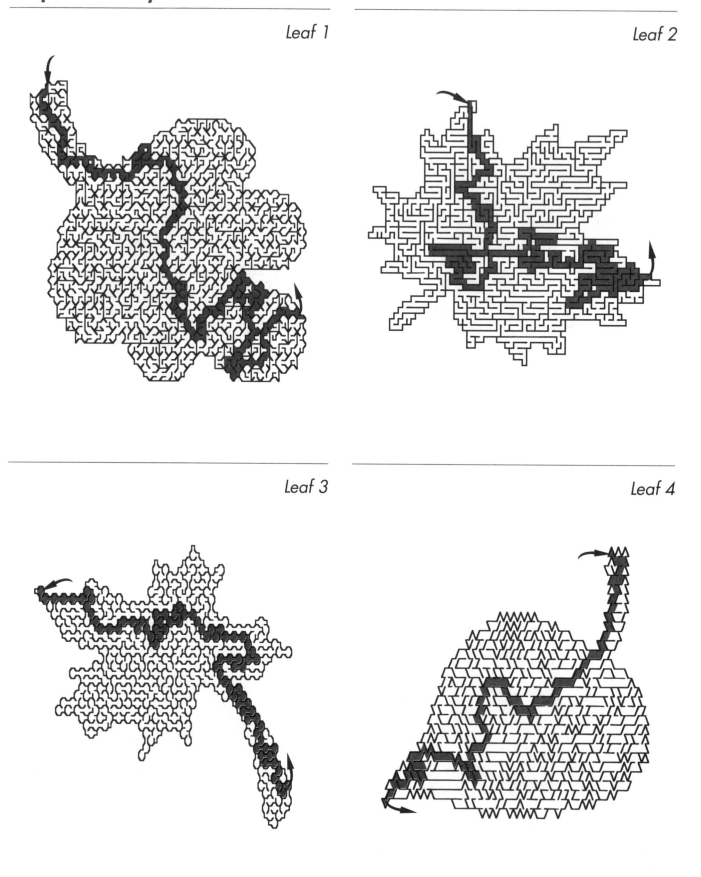

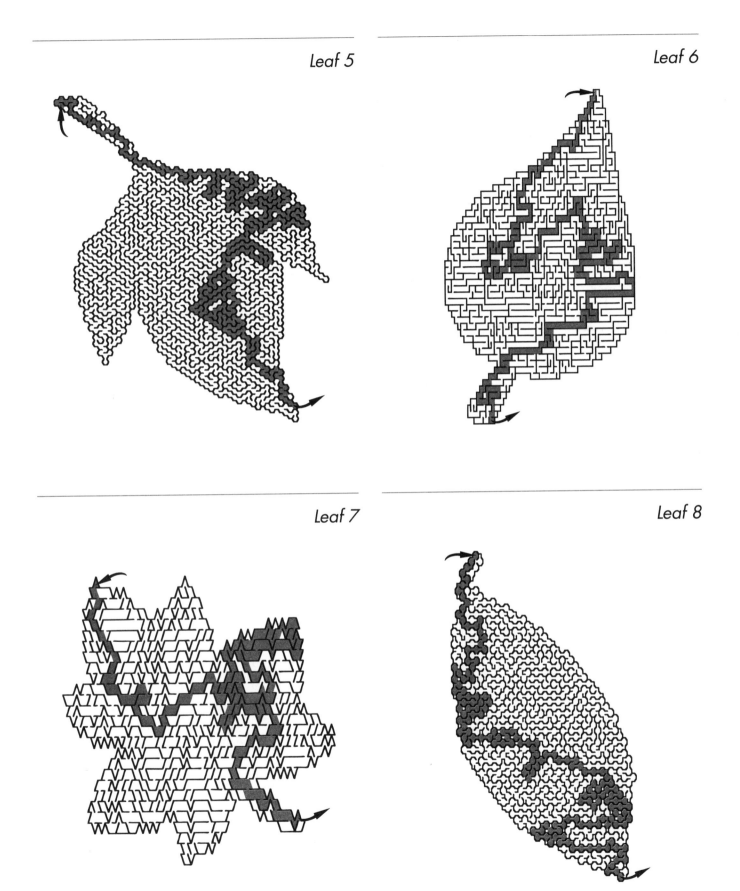

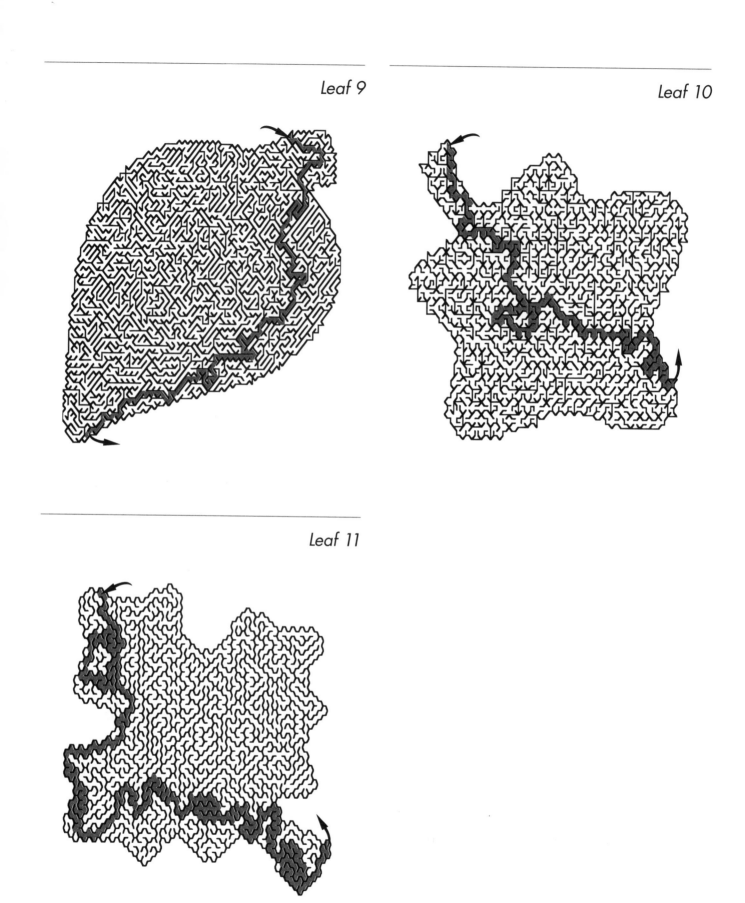

appendix b:
Maze Web Sites

Labyrinth Resource Centre

A fascinating website with history, photos, and Caerdroia: a journal about mazes and labyrinths.

✐ www.labyrinthos.net

Adrian Fisher Mazes

A leading designer of life-sized mazes made for castles, corn fields, and many other places around the world.

✐ www.mazemaker.com

Click Mazes

A cornucopia of unique mazes and interactive puzzles.

✐ www.clickmazes.com

Logic Mazes

Mazes with rules. Logical reasoning is required to make your way through these mazes.

✐ www.logicmazes.com

Puzzle Beast

A collection of mazes and puzzles including the Meandering Monk Maze.

✐ www.puzzlebeast.com

Delorie Software Maze Generator

Create your own custom mazes online.

✐ www.delorie.com/game-room/mazes

Maze, by Christopher Manson

Online version of the book. Move from room to room trying to solve this hyper-linked maze.

✐ archives.obs-us.com/obs/english/books/
holt/books/maze/

3-D Perspective Maze

Run around an online maze trying to find the exit.

✐ www.falstad.com/maze

Discovery School's Maze Puzzlemaker

Online software to create your own mazes. Brought to you by the Discovery Channel.

✐ puzzlemaker.school.discovery.com/
AdvMazeSetupForm.html

Mazes+Cartoons=Mazoons

A fun collection of maze cartoons that you can print.

✐ www.mazoons.com/Mazes.htm

Funster

A popular web site with word games and other puzzles created by the author of this book.

✐ www.funster.com

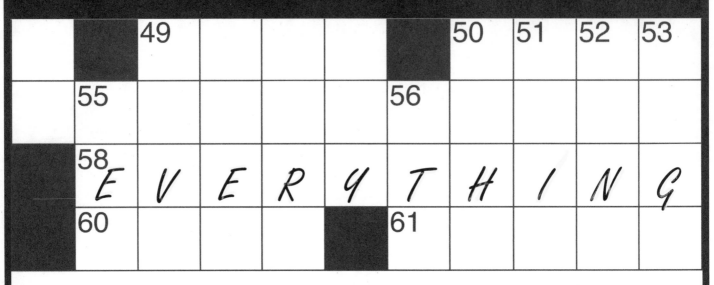